BEFORE THEY'RE GONE

BEFORE THEY'RE
GONE

A Family's Year-Long Quest to
Explore America's
Most Endangered National Parks

MICHAEL LANZA

Beacon Press • Boston

BEACON PRESS
25 Beacon Street
Boston, Massachusetts 02108-2892
www.beacon.org

Beacon Press books
are published under the auspices of
the Unitarian Universalist Association of Congregations.

15 14 13 12   8 7 6 5 4 3 2 1

This book is printed on acid-free paper that meets the uncoated paper
ANSI/NISO specifications for permanence as revised in 1992.

FRONTISPIECE
Gunsight Lake and, in the distance, Gunsight Pass, in Glacier National Park, Montana.

Text design by Wilsted & Taylor Publishing Services

Library of Congress Cataloging-in-Publication Data
Lanza, Michael.
Before they're gone : a family's year-long quest to explore America's
most endangered national parks / by Michael Lanza.
    p. cm.
Includes bibliographical references.
ISBN 978-0-8070-0119-6 (alk. paper)
1. National parks and reserves—Environmental aspects—United States.
2. Outdoor recreation—United States. 3. Family recreation—United States.
4. Climatic changes—United States. 5. Environmental degradation—
United States. 6. United States—Environmental conditions. I. Title.
E160.L367 2012
333.720973—dc23   2011039419

To my parents, for the gift of unconditional love.
To Penny, for understanding.
And to Nate and Alex, for teaching me.

The most beautiful thing we can experience is the mysterious. It is the source of all true art and all science. He to whom this emotion is a stranger, who can no longer pause to wonder and stand rapt in awe, is as good as dead: his eyes are closed.

—Albert Einstein

Unless someone like you cares a whole awful lot, nothing is going to get better. It's not.

—Dr. Seuss, from *The Lorax*

CONTENTS

PROLOGUE   Inspiration   xi

CHAPTER 1   Deepest Earth   1

CHAPTER 2   How Does the Water Go Up the Mountain?   19

CHAPTER 3   The Distant Rumble of White Thunder   37

CHAPTER 4   In the Long Shadow of "The Mountain"   55

CHAPTER 5   Along a Wild Coast   73

CHAPTER 6   The Backbone of the World   89

CHAPTER 7   If a Tree Falls   107

CHAPTER 8   Searching for Dr. Seuss   125

CHAPTER 9   The End of Winter   141

CHAPTER 10   Going Under   159

              Epilogue   177

              Acknowledgments   183

              Sources   187

PROLOGUE: INSPIRATION

The wind above ten thousand feet sweeps down from the cliffs, the August snowfields, and the jagged mountaintops high above us in gusts powerful enough to push around two hikers who each weigh less than my loaded backpack. The trail zigzags relentlessly upward, crossing a tilted sea of rocks that are embarked on an inexorable journey downhill, many of them advancing a little farther under our footsteps. The alpine sun bears down on these shadeless heights in Wyoming's Teton Range, and the air grows thin.

I check my two undersized companions for hints of fatigue, hunger, or unhappiness—a slowing pace, a faraway look, complaining. But none of these discomforts that would unhinge most adults appears to disturb my kids in the least.

Ahead of me walks Nate, eight years old and already a seasoned backpacker with several trips under his belt going back to age five—or to infancy, if you count the times he rode in a backpack. He absently swings Flipper, the stuffed dolphin in his hand, while discoursing, in elaborate detail and without pause, on his latest ideas for inventions: personal rockets powered by renewable energy and a device to make clouds shed more snow in winter—for skiing, of course.

Alex, our six-year-old daughter out on her most ambitious hike to date—eighteen miles over three days, including yesterday's climb of nearly 3,000 feet, and the 10,700-foot pass still above us, Paintbrush Divide—occasionally speaks to her stuffed dog, Swiss. Mostly, though, she passes the time playing our "number game," in which she and I try to guess what number we're each thinking of. She can play this game for hours without tiring of it. I'm getting a little tired of it. But it keeps her moving happily, if ploddingly forward, so I keep playing.

In everyday life, with its distractions and obligations, there exists no corollary for this time with them. In civilization, we race from one task to the next and fill our "leisure" time with programmed entertainment or the electronics and toys we've amassed. But in the backcountry, there's no daily planner. Beyond the needs of setting up camp and preparing food, there's nothing to demand our time except one another and the calmingly unscheduled live theater of nature. Only out here do I spend hours a day just talking to my wife and kids.

Since we started hiking yesterday morning, other backpackers have stopped and stared at our kids, asking their ages. Alex and Nate have probably noticed that we've seen only a few other kids out here. But they have no grasp of the anomaly of their own presence. It would mean nothing to them to hear that I was past thirty when I first saw these mountains and walked this trail; they are Westerners, but I was a child of the East who discovered the West as an adult. They don't yet appreciate that they are experiencing one of America's most beloved landscapes more intimately than the vast majority of their countrymen ever will.

But that's the problem with mature perspective: you don't acquire it until long after it first would have been useful.

Nate and Alex pause on an outcropping of broken rock. The land before us displays a sort of topographical bipolarity—plunging into a canyon bottom beyond our line of sight, then just as abruptly vaulting up into the impregnable fortress of rock walls and buttresses composing Mount Moran. This is something like my fifteenth trip in the Tetons, and yet familiarity has not dulled my awe of them. But my kids are not gushing over the scenery; they're pointing with amazement at a small tarn a couple hundred feet below us, still mostly ice-covered in mid-August. I know they ache to stand on its shore hurling stones to smash the ice.

As we near the pass, the wind musters even more force and the rocky, narrow trail clings to the face of a crumbling cliff. My wife, Penny, and I, with our longtime friend Bill Mistretta, hover close to our undaunted kids, herding them to the inside of the trail, away from the precipice. And we try to exude calm, as if we're just crossing the street to their elementary school.

Although preoccupied with my children's safety, I cannot help but notice—similar to what other Teton habitués have observed—that these mountains are less white in summer now than when I first backpacked and climbed here almost two decades ago. The planet grows steadily warmer. As in most mountain ranges, less of winter's snowfall survives through the summer here. The reverberations of this change echo around the world. But unlike a true echo, this one does not cease and its volume keeps rising.

Later that afternoon, we find a campsite by the swift creek pouring over steplike ledges in the North Fork of Cascade Canyon. I assume Alex and Nate will be exhausted from today's efforts. But they spend most of the hours until dark tirelessly tossing sticks into the foaming current or using the sticks to pound rocks, seeing serious purpose in missions that exist only in their imaginations. I see purpose in their activities, too. But I think the end product *is* imagination, and it all seems to begin with some ancient hardwiring in us to make tools.

WALKING IN THESE MOUNTAINS again stirs in me an upwelling of memories. Mental images glide like creek waters around the fixed midstream rocks anchoring me in the present: my kids. And yet, recollections remain viscerally vivid, retrieving sensations across years.

On a vertiginous wall a thousand feet above the cracked, wizened complexion of a glacier, my hands clutched rock that felt like a wrought-iron fence on a November morning, and I nervously watched clouds boiling up around pointy granite fingers overhead, hoping they wouldn't coalesce into thunderheads before we finished the climb. My skis whispered secrets knowable only to my two companions and me as we glided over snow that bore no evidence of other humans, and in every direction white mountains lunged for heaven and canyons collapsed into unseen depths. Water offered gentle resistance to the pull of my paddle tugging our canoe across a sun-warmed lake, its far shore sprouting a row of peaks resembling cathedrals. Leg muscles thickened and feet throbbed at the end of a twenty-mile day hike or a six-thousand-foot scramble, as a friend and I clinked bottles of beer and watched the setting sun perform the impossible, transforming water vapor impaled upon mountaintops into flames.

Invariably, people occupy these memories, imbuing them with the broadest dimension: emotion.

Powerful landscapes like the Tetons will manhandle your psyche; they can make you wonder what the hell you've been doing all these years, for which you won't have a satisfying answer. But overlaying a complex tapestry of personal history on a place of aching natural beauty animates it. In time, the place insinuates itself into a major role in the story of your life.

I've tasted the purest distillations of peacefulness and joy, hardship and sorrow in the Tetons. Amid scenery reached only through exhausting effort, I've laughed with my closest friends, one of whom died on another mountain far from here. Returning to ground where Rick and I stood together years ago inevitably resurrects memories that make me smile. But I also feel his absence, like I'm in an empty room where we were supposed to meet.

I once shuffled five miles in dizzying pain from a foot broken in a fall while scrambling off a peak—and yet the rock climb that preceded the fall was so wonderful it still overshadows that day's disaster in my mind. I've narrowly escaped off a peak after my ice ax hummed through a violent electrical storm, and peered at a bull elk standing right outside our tents in the milky glow of a full moon. I've stumbled upon a solo climber injured in a fall, initiating his rescue, and trembled at discovering what remained of another who had plunged five hundred feet onto talus. I've hiked with a friend in otherwise absolute solitude through terrain where wind raised whitecaps on emerald lakes below temples of geology.

And Penny and I first visited this park together sixteen years ago, before marriage, during a summer of hiking and climbing around the

West when we lived for three months in a cramped tent and an aging Honda Civic packed to the ceiling and windows with gear.

For me, the Tetons are a box jammed with memories. Virtually every trail, campsite, and summit here murmurs at least one tale. Hearing them again, I smile, wince, or feel as deeply as ever a great loss—as if these events, some recent and some bubbling up from long ago, stand together just over my shoulder, oblivious to the creep of time.

Being here with my kids feels like watching them play in the house where I grew up. So I think the thrill hits me as intensely as it does Alex and Nate when, walking down Cascade Canyon in warm sunshine on our final afternoon, we come up on two big bull moose, their huge racks nodding up and down as they graze in the sparse forest fifty feet from us.

Watching those moose, I wonder what my kids will not experience because of the slow, warm flood inundating nature.

TWO YEARS EARLIER, IN the first days of April 2007, on assignment to write an article for *Backpacker Magazine*, I skied high into the Northern Rockies of Montana's Glacier National Park with federal scientist Dan Fagre, who had sounded the warning that the seven-thousand-year-old glaciers in one of America's most revered parks would be gone within a human generation. Amid snow-covered peaks rising above nine thousand feet along the Continental Divide, one degree of latitude south of the Canadian border, we skied into a wilderness seen by perhaps a handful of people each year outside the short summer season.

At the trip's outset, we saw something that shocked even the dispassionate veteran scientist Fagre: bare ground. A March "heat wave" of 60 degree temperatures had melted away four feet of snowpack in a place that doesn't normally see the mercury climb that high until July. We hiked for several miles with our skis on our backpacks before getting high enough to reach snow.

That story assignment ignited a personal interest in the impacts of global warming on the natural world. The science fascinated me. I found it disturbing, but it also captivated me in the way that my favorite science-fiction books had as a boy. These reports of ongoing change and projections of the future climate read less like dry science than biblical cataclysm: massive floods and lahars; the collapse of gigantic ice shelves; world-famous mountains raining tons of rock onto climbers; mass extinctions of species on a scale unseen in two hundred million years; and enormous rivers of ice racing eighty feet per day to break up in the sea, or retreating sixty-five miles in the blink of a geologic eye.

I saw symptoms of this epidemic just about everywhere I went hiking and climbing: dried-up, cracked earth where a mountain lake had rippled in the wind just a few summers before, and peaks whose distribution of glacial ice, alpine lakes, meadows, and forest looked nothing like what was shown on our map. I saw bizarrely warm January afternoons on ten-thousand-foot peaks that are usually encased in bitter cold at that time of year, and abnormally hot summer days in mountains that have long offered refuge from the heat.

In summer 2007, hiking in the Tetons, I saw that a perennial snowfield on the Middle Teton, known to generations of climbers, had dried up. And just a few weeks before my arrival, climbers inside a tent pitched high in Garnet Canyon—a spot where I had camped thirteen years earlier, on my first attempt to climb the 13,770-foot Grand Teton— heard the clatter of falling rocks in the darkness around them. As the fusillade increased, they fled their tent. Moments later, a massive rock slide obliterated their campsite.

In the Tetons and in ranges around the world, rising temperatures are melting the permafrost, the year-round ice and snow that acts as glue in big mountains, holding everything frozen together. Lose that, and rocks begin falling with alarming frequency, occasionally with deadly results. In 2003, in an incident that probably made headlines on every continent, more than seventy climbers were rescued off the Matterhorn following a series of massive rockfalls, compelling officials to temporarily close one of world's most famous peaks.

Rocks fall off mountains, snow melts in summer—those stories are as old as waves crashing on beaches. But short of a volcanic eruption or some other cataclysm, mountains are not supposed to change so dramatically, so suddenly. These events are not freak occurrences; they are bellwethers of the tectonic shifts tearing through the natural world, wrought by forces we have set in motion but which now possess a momentum of their own.

In a fleeting century and a half of industrialization, we have weirdly recalibrated nature. My kids' formative years will roughly coincide with our society's maturation on climate change: they were born around the time that we finally began to widely acknowledge its impacts, and they will reach adulthood as we are likely to begin witnessing its full fallout.

I wonder whether they will sound like people of my generation when we reminisce about how much more snow fell and how ponds froze over for ice skating in the winters of our childhoods. Will my kids look upon the Earth—which could become several degrees hotter than when their grandparents were born—with the wiser, more analytical perspective demanded of their generation?

How do I explain to a nine-year-old and a seven-year-old that humanity—mostly their parents' and grandparents' generations—has behaved in such a shortsighted way that these parks we're visiting will look and feel very different by the time they are my age?

TWO WEEKS AFTER OUR wedding (on D-day 1998), Penny and I moved from New England to Idaho—two more Easterners imagining ourselves adopting the West, but gradually understanding that it has adopted us. Probably like many uprooted Americans, I feel more connected to personal history and to the scattered places where I've written it than to any region or ethnic heritage. Now it deeply disturbed me to consider what this mounting climate upheaval portended for places that store pieces of my history, which I hope to bequeath to my children.

Yosemite's famous waterfalls—which I've walked beneath during times of high runoff, when the spray hit hikers like a fire hose—will lose their impressive force and peter out earlier in the year as average temperatures continue climbing. Alaska's premier sea kayaking destination, Glacier Bay National Park—where long tongues of ice descend from snowbound mountains to lap at the sea, calving bus-size icebergs into waters teeming with seals, fish, and killer whales—has seen the fastest glacial retreat on the planet. Rising seas will inundate at least one-third of Olympic National Park's seventy-three-mile-long wilderness coastline, where I've tottered across tree trunks stripped of their bark and branches by the tide and left heaped on the beach.

Across the continent, much of Florida's Everglades, one of Earth's greatest sanctuaries of biological diversity, appears fated to sink beneath the waves. Joshua Tree National Park, where I've rock climbed the famously fingertip-shredding granite towers, will lose its namesake flora. In Yellowstone, long one of the nation's iceboxes, with some of the coldest temperatures in the Lower 48—a park where I've skied among geysers and watched wolves pursue stampeding elk—winter is, incredibly, shrinking.

In civilization, it's easy to ignore the changes because we've created insular living environments. We simply run the air conditioning or lawn sprinklers a little more. But nature is responding in myriad, complex ways that scientists say include bigger storms and wildfires, growing infestations of exotic plants and insects, rising sea levels—and the sixth and fastest mass extinction of life on Earth. We're in the midst of a holocaust that is expected to claim up to 40 percent of plant and animal species worldwide by 2100, including 21 percent of mammals, 37 percent of freshwater fish, and 70 percent of plants.

The scope and depth of what's occurring, like a hurricane leaving nothing untouched, struck me as an ironic tragedy, in that it's overhauling our most-protected natural environments. The places we've diligently set aside to preserve in their pristine condition in perpetuity are reeling under ecological calamities triggered by global warming and frequently magnified by physical dynamics that escalate out of control. It seems unbelievable, but these parks will be profoundly changed in a human generation or two. Within a century and a half of the founding of Yellowstone, which introduced the national park concept to the world, we are undermining one of mankind's greatest achievements.

We've designated and protected national parks because we need these places. They inspire us. They bring out our best as individuals and represent our highest aspirations as a civilization. They express our humility, our ability to step outside ourselves and acknowledge the inherent worth of leaving distinctive pieces of our world alone, instead of measuring their value only in resources we can consume, as humans have done over much of the Earth's surface.

Climate change raises a new take on the old philosophical question of the tree falling in the forest: if the last few square feet of a seven-thousand-year-old glacier melt into the dirt and we don't care, did it matter?

I know many of these places intimately. They compose the backdrop to much of the narrative of my life. For years, I've compiled a growing to-do list of adventures I want to enjoy with my family, hopefully inspiring Alex and Nate to someday repeat these trips with their own kids. What a wonderful legacy, I thought.

Now carbon dioxide was messing with my plans. It seemed I needed to get busy.

IN THE COLD, DARKENING weeks of late autumn 2009, an idea began taking shape: embarking on wilderness adventures with my family in as many climate-threatened U.S. national parks as we could cram into a year.

It was not, of course, the last year to see these places before some climate cataclysm. And the motivation was about more than that—it was about sharing these experiences with our kids. Plus, the changes taking place, the rising seas, melting ice, and dwindling snowpack, are occurring not on a geologic time scale, but on a human one. If Glacier National Park's glaciers are diminishing almost every summer, should we wait even five years?

Penny and I had long, skeptical discussions about the wisdom of taking nine- and seven-year-old kids backpacking among grizzly bears in Glacier, or paddling among alligators in the Everglades, or sea kayaking in Glacier Bay, where orcas patrol waters cold enough to suck the life from an adult in fifteen minutes. We understand the ruthlessness of the outdoors. Fifteen years ago, she and I labored side by side trying, and failing, to resuscitate our good friend Rick after a climbing accident.

But life doesn't extend opportunities indefinitely, waiting for us to grab them. In a few years, Alex and Nate will be teenagers, consumed with their own interests. They may be harder to persuade to take long, arduous wilderness journeys with their annoying parents. Many people make a vow to accomplish a goal eventually, only to realize years later that their promise has eluded fulfillment, sacrificed to career, family, inertia. I didn't want to someday have to gnaw on that indigestible kernel of regret.

Then in early December 2009, as Penny and I were having these conversations, the World Meteorological Organization announced that the first decade of the twenty-first century was very likely the warmest on record. That came on the heels of the 1990s, which had a string of the warmest years on record.

The signs all pointed in the same direction.

My plan was feasible, if at times hectic. The eleven adventures I had in mind lent themselves to a nicely rhythmic seasonal progression: backpacking into the Grand Canyon in early spring; hiking to Yosemite's waterfalls at their peak in early summer; sea kayaking in Alaska's Glacier Bay and backpacking in the North Cascades, in the wildflower meadows of Mount Rainier, on the Olympic coast, and in Montana's Glacier National Park at the height of summer; catching the golden explosion of Colorado's aspens in early autumn; rock climbing during the mild days of midautumn in the desert of Joshua Tree National Park; and cross-country skiing in Yellowstone and paddling the subtropical Everglades in winter. Seven of those eleven parks are UNESCO World Heritage Sites, selected for their unique natural beauty and biological value.

Beyond questions of safety, I worried somewhat about how much we would all enjoy these adventures, none of which would be easy. The wilderness can be miserable at times even for adults. I might be setting myself up for hearing a heap of high-pitched complaining.

IN ANOTHER TIME, IN a life long before this one, I lived to the age of thirty-nine years, four months, and twenty-seven days childless. Then my son arrived. I didn't notice it at the time, probably because I wasn't paying close enough attention, but when he entered my life, he closed a door behind himself.

My daughter came along a month before I turned forty-two. Like most parents, I had no advance warning of, no idea of, how hard it can be. I had many days at home solo with an infant and toddler when I'd look at the clock and realize, with crushing disappointment, that only minutes had passed since I last looked at it. I had coasted childless through two adult decades, afloat in that freedom from the hardest responsibility; and frankly, for a long time, I really missed that lifestyle.

But a hole in your life is like any hole—emptiness remains invisible until you fill it in. So it was for me with becoming a father.

I've now reached an age, statistically beyond life's midway point, when time seems to be something I'm no longer adding up so much as counting down. Although, with luck, there's plenty of it left, I no longer have the luxury of running down the clock. That realization can inspire a compelling urge to do something right. For most of us, the best possible contribution we can make to the world is raising people who, at the least, don't mess things up more.

I want my kids to discover what I've found: the satisfying simplicity of purpose in moving under your own power, at human velocity, through a place crowded not with people, artificial noise, machines, or flashing lights, but with the abundance of nature. I've seen how a rushing creek, a mountain lake, or a pine forest engages my kids endlessly, never bores them like our yard or the school playground. Like adults, they find something intangible but necessary in the complexity and stimulation of a natural environment, something that's missing from the manufactured environs where we live. I hope to paint for Nate and Alex a larger picture of the world and educate them about climate change, but mostly to sear into them memories that outlive Penny and me.

My work as an outdoor writer and photographer gives me an excuse to go out on adventures in places like Patagonia, Iceland, New Zealand, and many U.S. national parks. For most of the year, though, I lead a very ordinary life. I work at home, and with a wife who's a family doctor, I function as the parent who gets our kids off to school in the morning and is waiting for them when school lets out; who gets them to soccer practice, dentist appointments, and music lessons; who volunteers (mostly with moms) in their classrooms; who bikes with them to the library and barber shop and prepares most of our dinners.

It's a bit of a schizophrenic lifestyle, and the best one I've worked out so far.

So I suppose it was inevitable that a story that consumed me, about national parks and climate change, would eventually meld with my biggest responsibility—that the two small people whose needs and laughter fill my typical days would become part of that story.

Although I'm telling it, it's more their story than mine. Whatever becomes of our changing world, they have to live in it.

This book only begins a much longer tale. My kids will own its ending.

I believe they will take away much good from this year of adventure. Maybe they'll even communicate to their generation a vision for a more realistic relationship between people and our world, and the moral imperative of not ignoring the fact that we're broiling our planet under the hot lamp of selfish indifference. In spite of the overwhelming weight of science, we've failed to gather the momentum of honesty required to do what is necessary and right. So I take my kids on this year-long journey in part because I wonder whether my generation possesses the collective humility to save us from ourselves.

But mostly, I'm doing this year outdoors for my kids—and, certainly, for Penny and me. For joy, curiosity, and wonder. Because I want my kids to see these things before they're gone.

John Muir said, "In every walk with nature one receives far more than he seeks."

That's exactly what I hope we'll find.

ON A LATE NOVEMBER afternoon in Boise, as we grow impatient waiting for overdue snowstorms to whiten the mountains and announce the ski season, a letter arrives in the mail from Grand Canyon National Park. It's a permit to backpack at the end of March, our kids' spring break. It follows two rejections of earlier applications this fall in the lottery free-for-all for one of the world's most sought-after wilderness permits. So I trumpet this good news to Penny and the kids, building the anticipation as I like to do.

Then I take a deep breath and let it slowly out.

BEFORE THEY'RE GONE

Alex hikes past a beavertail cactus on the Tonto East Trail in the
Grand Canyon, Arizona, with Zoroaster Temple in the distance.

CHAPTER 1

DEEPEST EARTH

MARCH 2010

In a lifetime spent making many thousands of decisions, we get a mulligan on most of them. It's the rare judgment call that's final, where you get no second chance. You don't want to blow one of those.

I stop and stare at the trail ahead of us with the feeling like I've recently eaten something I shouldn't have. Little more than a foot wide and plastered in hardpacked snow and ice, it clings to the face of a cliff with a drop-off of hundreds of feet. It evokes a ledge outside a skyscraper window on the eightieth floor, in a northern city locked in winter. At the trail's narrowest point, the cliff bulges outward, as if the rock wall had a conscious desire to hip-check us into the yawning abyss of the Grand Canyon.

It's hard for me to look at this and *not* form a disconcerting mental image of pitching off, free-falling past layers of rock hundreds of millions of years old, tumbling figuratively back in time until my own time terminates abruptly somewhere way down there. I stomp my boots yet again into the firm snow, testing the grip of the microspikes, miniature crampons with half-inch metal points attached to the outsoles. I'm placing a lot of faith in them. But it's not me that I'm worried about.

I look down at my seven-year-old daughter, Alex. At four feet tall and fifty pounds a thin-limbed wisp of a child, she believes to her marrow that her dad, squeezing her hand reassuringly, will guide her safely around that corner—and the next, and the next, and over however

1

many icy precipices lie ahead on our descent of the Grandview Trail, which zigzags across wildly exposed ledges on its three-thousand-foot drop into the Big Ditch.

This trail's scary even in ideal conditions, when it's dry. Unlike Grand Canyon National Park's tourist herd paths, the Bright Angel and South Kaibab trails, the Grandview Trail doesn't attract a steady parade of people. Most would turn back at the first glimpse of this dizzying exposure.

But now, in late March, sheathed in snow that has softened and refrozen every day and night and been compacted by the boots of the occasional hikers venturing down here, it has nearly the hardness of a skating rink. A park ranger we spoke with this morning had grimly called this goat path "very treacherous."

In the clench of Alex's small hand, I can feel nervousness and trust. I've felt it before and seen her resolve when she rock climbed beside me 150 feet up a granite cliff for the first time, cross-country skied through a blizzard to a backcountry yurt, and shared a two-person kayak with me paddling down Utah's Green River—the latter two adventures when she was four. Now just a week past her seventh birthday, this girl has seen more adventure than most Americans do in a lifetime. But I don't think I've ever felt as anxious about her safety as I do right now.

I can't help wonder, Do parents whose children spend five hours a day in front of an electronic screen ever grapple with the judgment call vexing me now: is this *really* a good idea?

I have already contemplated turning back, aborting our four-day, twenty-nine-mile backpacking trip just an hour into it. But I have already walked that ledge across and back again to test how slick it is and to leave my backpack on the other side, and then led my nine-year-old son, Nate, around it. My wife, Penny, now waits around the corner with Nate. In circumstances like this, she often trusts our children's safety to my judgment—something that I always find gratifying and astounding, while knowing it comes with an implied caveat: don't mess up, bub. Our friends from back home in Boise, Jeff Wilhelm and his seventeen-year-old daughter, Jasmine, wait their turn on that traverse.

The difference on this walk across that icy ledge is that while I had microspikes that fit Nate's boots, I don't have a pair small enough for Alex's. If she slips, I'll be holding one skinny wrist to keep her grounded.

So I smile and wink at Alex and tell her to "take small steps and go slow." She nods and winks back—we have an understanding. We shuffle forward. With my free hand, I clutch scrawny plants tenuously rooted to cracks in the crumbly cliff face. A minute crawls past like an epoch. We round the corner to where the trail widens and becomes less exposed. Penny says, "Nice job, Alex," and offers me a smile. I exhale a two-lung load of relief.

If nothing ahead of us is worse than that, we'll be fine. I think.

"What took you so long?" Nate asks.

How do I answer that one? I refrain from lecturing him about relative hazards and consequences. I don't bother pointing out the certainty of death in the event of a slip off that ledge. And there seems no point explaining how leading Alex and him across it cut a deep and wide gash into my primal instinct to avoid placing one's genetic legacy in peril. I sense all this might be lost on my nine-year-old.

Just two and a half years older than his sister, my son sees himself as an expert in multiple disciplines, a wilderness/Renaissance boy sewn together with swatches from the souls of Thomas Jefferson and Ernest Shackleton. It no longer surprises me. Overconfidence cruises the uncertain terrain of boyhood, as indigenous to it as a fascination with weaponry and an indifference to changing your clothes daily. I recall those clumsy, stumbling years with a mix of mortification and nostalgic yearning for such blissful ignorance. The greatest burden of maturity is knowing how often you're wrong.

But like most families, mine never ventured down icy Grand Canyon footpaths. My suburban youth's greatest hazards were bullies and falling within range of a buddy's BB gun or a firecracker—both scarier to me then than these trails seem to Nate today.

I heave my pack onto my back and promise Nate that I'll try harder to keep up. And we continue on to the next frozen catwalk.

SWALLOWED UP BY THE canyon's immensity and severe relief, in the space of two hours we ride the icy escalator of terror down 2,500 feet, stepping from snow onto dry dirt and rock, from winter into summer. We shed jackets and expressions of consternation to hike in T-shirts under a crushing sense of insignificance.

Before us unfolds one of the world's most magnificent landscapes and greatest visual deceptions. Its name should be plural. Millions of years of erosion have incised not one canyon but a confounding labyrinth 277 miles long and up to fifteen miles wide and six thousand feet deep, scored by about three hundred twisting side canyons, some of them several miles long and thousands of feet deep. The national park, a World Heritage Site, covers more than 1.2 million acres and encompasses five of the planet's seven life zones. Roughly the size of Delaware, it mirrors the breadth of biological diversity spanning the United States from Mexico to Canada.

The Grand Canyon turns earth inside out, exposing its guts. It's an open book of geologic history dating back nearly 1.8 billion years, to Precambrian time, before the first known life forms existed on Earth; no fossils have been found in the oldest rock of the Inner Gorge, the erosion-resistant Vishnu Schist. But fossils abound in most of the nearly forty named layers of rock stacked from newest to oldest as one moves downward, from the uppermost and youngest Kaibab Limestone to the billion-year-old Kwagunt Formation and deeper. These stone tablets tell of ancient, shallow seas and a long-ago desert, and of the creatures that wandered through them. Plot a time line of the history of our genus, *Homo,* against the geologic history displayed in the Grand Canyon, and the contrast would be roughly equivalent to comparing the height of a seven-foot-tall man standing beside the Colorado River to the height of the South Rim, a vertical mile overhead.

It taxes comprehension, this vastness of sheer walls and steep, crumbling slopes stacked in neat layers of rust-red, dirty orange, creamy white, muddy brown, and black, with daubs of green; the array of overlapping chasms and castlelike buttes and towers; the long shadows that lend this space infinite depth. With so little vegetation, the land appears stripped nearly bare, so emaciated that its stone bones bulge against its thin skin of soil. With almost limitless views, your eyes pan slowly over everything and your brain picks through its files for the memory of something similar to put this scene in context, but there's no box it will fit inside.

We've come to the Big Ditch during perhaps its most schizophrenic season: early spring, when the climatic chasm separating the canyon bottom from the rims seems most pronounced.

In the canyon's deep basement, a scorched land 2,500 feet above sea level that receives about eight inches of rain a year—as much as the Gobi Desert—daytime highs already reach 60 to 70 degrees Fahrenheit. Spring is feeling rather randy down there: streams pregnant with runoff from snowmelt, flowers lusting for pollination, birds chirping songs of reproduction.

But winter clings tenaciously to the canyon rims, a vertical mile and more above the river. A sugary coating of new snow will suddenly dust red rock, as it did just a few days before we arrived. The relentless, abrasive wind will scrape the nose off your face and rattle your skeleton with shivers. The rims still feel as far from springtime as Mexicali from British Columbia.

The Grand Canyon presents a dilemma to hikers: There's no ideal time of year temperature-wise. The thermometer will vary 30 to 40 degrees between the rim and the inner canyon at any given time and from day to night in any location. With daytime highs over 90 and 100 degrees Fahrenheit, summer is for reptiles and fools. Mid-autumn is a popular time, beyond summer's killing heat and before the snows have accumulated; but days are short and can deliver cold wind, unseasonal heat, or an early snowfall—perhaps all three. In winter, frigid winds pound canyon rims encased in snow, while direct sunlight rarely splashes the inner canyon because its walls are so high and the sun so low.

Many backpackers come in midspring, but there's a short window between when the snow has departed from the rims and the interior grows unbearably hot. Penny and I reminisce now about learning that lesson the last time we dropped off the South Rim, sixteen months before the confident boy charging ahead of us was born, when six of us backpacked for four days in May through withering heat.

Experiencing the canyon has always demanded considerable toil, in the informed opinion of John Wesley Powell, the one-armed Civil War veteran who led the first expedition down the Colorado River through the Grand Canyon in 1869. He wrote, "You cannot see the Grand Canyon in one view, as if it were a changeless spectacle from which a curtain might be lifted, but to see it you have to toil from month to month through its labyrinths." Few who have done so would argue with Powell.

It seems inevitable that the Big Ditch will become only more difficult to explore, especially on foot, in the warmer climate of coming years.

WE FOLLOW THE TRAIL across Horseshoe Mesa, 2,500 feet below where we started hiking at Grandview Point and 2,400 feet above the Colorado River. All around us, soaring buttes extend for miles like crooked fingers off the South and North rims, casting heavy, lengthening shadows as afternoon drips quietly into evening. In this severe, convoluted topography, nightfall doesn't drop like a curtain. The drama stretches across a few hours, with Rorschach pools of gray spreading sluggishly over the ground, until they connect in one solid shadow; and then the glowing coals of last sunlight on the tallest formations die out to silhouettes against the stars.

Far down to our left, I can see tonight's destination, Cottonwood Creek—the first water source along a route where, as with any multiday trip in this sere place, scarce creeks and springs dictate where you camp, eat, and *always* refill your bottles. Shadow has already overtaken that side canyon, and it's still a thousand vertical feet and nearly two miles away on a tortuous trail that constantly presents broken stones, gravel like ball bearings, and big steps down off ledges.

I imagine it's only harder if you're four feet tall.

Finally, near the tail end of the prolonged dusk, we reach the creek and pitch tents beneath plump cottonwood trees. Beyond the campsite's compacted earth, an obstacle course of sagebrush and thorny plants rises steeply to a horseshoe of red cliffs enclosing this side canyon. Forgetting his fatigue, Nate gravitates to the stream. Alex migrates opportunistically between Penny's lap and mine.

We eat pasta with pesto by the electric candlelight of headlamps. With Jeff, a college English professor, kayaker, and recreational Nordic ski racer; and Jasmine, an astonishingly centered teenager and, as Penny and I would vouch, one of America's great babysitters, we talk late into the night about skiing (Penny also races), books, movies, politics, social media—a universe of entertainment lights up when conversation becomes the default form. Our voices lift through the dry, still air toward a silent detonation of stars salting the inscrutable blackness.

DURING HIS 1869 EXPEDITION down the canyon, John Wesley Powell gushed effusively about springs in journal passages like this one:

> On coming nearer we find fountains bursting from the rock high overhead, and the spray in the sunshine forms the gems which bedeck the wall. The rocks below the fountain are covered with mosses and ferns and many beautiful flowering plants. We name it Vasey's Paradise.

If paradise is defined by the presence of water, such Edens occur rarely in the Grand Canyon. The canyon's great irony is that water created and shaped it, yet remains so scarce. This truth is a cruel joke that nature plays on those of us who would endeavor to follow Powell's advice to "toil . . . through its labyrinths."

Most of the canyon's annual precipitation falls in two seasons: either during the storms of winter or the regional "monsoon" of late summer, which is characterized by short, intense rainfalls. The South Rim averages sixteen inches of precipitation annually, the higher North Rim twenty-seven inches. Much of that falls as snow in both places. The plateaus surrounding the canyon are devoid of natural streams and lakes. All of the water falling to earth is absorbed by thirsty vegetation or quickly percolates down through the many crevices in the canyon's porous top layer, the Kaibab Limestone.

Eventually, that water hits a less-permeable layer, like the Hermit or Bright Angel Shale, flowing laterally over that solid rock until it emerges from a canyon wall somewhere as a spring or seep. There are twelve known types of springs worldwide; ten exist in the Grand Canyon, and each supports different complex microhabitats. These scattered trickles and aquatic eruptions could be called the veins and capillaries of the canyon, for without them, little would live here.

It's a wonder that anything does. The estimated six hundred springs and seeps in the Grand Canyon cover just one-hundredth of 1 percent of the park's area—but support one hundred to five hundred times more species than the surrounding desert. Many springs host flora and fauna found nowhere else, like two on the South Rim where the only known white-flowering redbud trees grow. Approaching these springs can create the disorienting impression of having blacked out and awakened elsewhere: you step from a virtually barren, quiet desert into an oasis where butterflies fill the air and the sounds of yellow warblers and tree frogs emerge from the lush greenery of cottonwoods, cattails, and sedges.

Researchers have discovered that monsoon rains have little effect on the flow from springs; but when snow begins melting, springs receive an enormous pulse of water. Up to three-fourths of water emerging from springs is snowmelt—suggesting that a hotter climate, with more rain instead of snow, does not bode well for springs and all that rely on them, from cottonwood trees to backpackers.

Nature plays another cruel joke on backpackers: water is a heavy substance, weighing a bit more than two pounds per liter. And unlike a camel or a cactus, we can't survive long without it. Hiking in the desert, we each need at least four liters per day. A painful calculation puts the water needs of my family at roughly thirty-four pounds—every day.

At this time of year, in spring, Cottonwood Creek sends a shallow flow toward the Colorado River. By summer, like many ephemeral streams in the canyon, it usually dries to a cracked bed of blowing dust. If we were to attempt this same hike in fall along these twenty-nine miles, in all likelihood only Grapevine Creek, in the next side canyon five miles beyond Cottonwood, would flow. For even the fittest backpackers, the added water load would make this trek significantly harder. For families with young kids, it might be impossible.

And dry-season conditions might become the new norm for the Grand Canyon of the future.

———

In the morning, after packing up camp, we walk a half hour along Cottonwood Creek to a trail junction. From here, we will leave the creek to follow the Tonto Trail's serpentine course westward across the broad, cacti-studded Tonto Plateau for more than two days, before climbing three thousand feet back up to the South Rim on our last day. Over the remaining twenty-four miles of hiking, we expect to find, at most, three sources of water—none on our final day.

Given that my kids can't carry more than a liter each, I try not to think about how much I'll have to haul for our last twenty-four hours out here, on top of the family gear and food already straining the seams of my pack.

As I crouch to fill bottles and purify the water with a chlorine-based solution, Nate and Alex stack stones nearby in a futile effort to dam the creek. We all celebrate water in our own way.

Then Nate comes up to me to say his pack's too heavy. He's carrying a real backpack for the first time—on previous trips, like Alex, he carried just a day pack with his own water. Containing his clothes, sleeping bag, and water, plus several ounces of stuffed-animal ballast, his pack weighs at least twelve pounds—a significant load for someone his size. I give him credit for carrying it this far without complaint, though he had told me halfway down the Grandview Trail yesterday, "Wow, I can't believe how hard it is."

I pull his sleeping bag from his pack and, with much rearranging and cramming, shoehorn it inside mine. An unhappy back is easier to deal with out here than an unhappy kid.

An hour beyond Cottonwood Creek, the trail leads us out to the raggedly torn-off edge of the Tonto Plateau, where the ground suddenly plunges over thousand-foot-tall cliffs into the Inner Gorge. In its bottom, the roiling, grittily chocolate Colorado River—which Powell described as "too thick to drink, to thin to plow" because of its heavy load of sediment—rumbles and hisses between walls of dark rock.

Turning around, we can see the buttresses and pyramidal towers of the South Rim, sprinkled in confectioner's sugar, miles and thousands of feet from us. Just yesterday we stood up there, watching a California condor glide overhead on its 13,000-year journey from the last ice age, when life was good for a carnivore that scavenged dead mammoths and mastodons. If the Grand Canyon looks unreal from the rim, its scale impossible to discern, down here in its belly, we reel through a perpetual optical illusion.

Miles become elastic. You walk but have little immediate impression of making progress because the rock formations are so large and lie at such distances that nothing appears to draw closer. Gradually, one monumental tower of stone inches toward us from the backdrop; it seems to expand like a slowly filling dirigible until it looms mountainous. As we pass by and continue beyond for hours, it shrinks backward one tiny step at a time. Then we turn around and it is gone. What was gigantic has evaporated, and something else ahead of us swells larger. In the Grand Canyon, you can see for miles but never perceive the true size of things.

Captain Garcia Lopez de Cardenas and his soldiers knew that illusion. In September 1540, they became the first Europeans to lay eyes on the Grand Canyon. Cardenas was under the command of the Spanish conquistador Francisco Vasquez de Coronado, who searched with a true believer's dauntless optimism for Cibola, a mythical city of gold. Seeing the Colorado River from the South Rim, the Spanish presumed it was a small stream, not far away, despite their Hopi guides' insistence that the river was indeed quite large and far off. Cardenas dispatched three men to find a way down, probably never imagining that the hole into which he sent them could become their grave. They returned a few days later parched and beaten, having gotten nowhere near the river, and reported that the rocks that appeared tiny from the rim stood as tall as the Tower of Seville.

We come to the rim of Grapevine Canyon, another manifestation of the elasticity of miles here. This Colorado tributary slices a sheer-walled chasm more than a thousand feet deep. We walk upstream along its rim to cross the slender stream at the point where it begins chopping into the Tonto Plateau. After an hour-long break to eat, refill bottles, and allow Nate and Alex time to engineer their notion of improvements to the creek's natural flow, we swing 180 degrees to follow the opposite rim—ultimately hiking more than five miles around Grapevine Canyon. At the far end of this U-shaped detour, I look back across Grape-vine's gaping mouth to a point of land less than a mile away, where we stood four hours ago.

Again, we walk into cool evening shadows. I can detect creeping exhaustion in both of the kids. Then Jasmine draws them into her orbit, distracting them from their weariness with conversation as we plod on-ward. It feels like everyone's tank is down to fumes when we end a long, ten-mile day, pitching camp on the open, sagebrush-covered plateau, in wind that would hurl our tents into the Inner Gorge if we didn't stake them securely to the ground.

Across the canyon, multi-tiered, three-thousand-foot-tall Zoroaster Temple cleaves the sky like a red war bonnet, and the sun's last rays soften the cliff tops of the North Rim. I wonder whether, ten millennia ago, people sat here and felt the same awe that we do tonight.

HUMANS HAVE WANDERED OR lived in virtually every corner of the Grand Canyon for more than ten thousand years. More than one hundred Native American routes into the canyon are known. The Anasazi and Cohonina peoples thrived for centuries, but vanished mysteriously in the late thirteenth century, probably fleeing drought. We may soon better understand their experience here.

The Colorado River basin has warmed more since the 1970s than anywhere else in the United States except Alaska. (For a variety of reasons owing to the complexities of climate, some parts of the globe are warming faster than others.) The average temperature from 2003 to 2007 was 2.2 degrees Fahrenheit hotter than the twentieth-century average. The region remains mired in its most severe drought in more than a century of record keeping—consistent with scientific projections that it will dry out more than any other part of the country.

The Intergovernmental Panel on Climate Change (IPCC), the Nobel Peace Prize–winning United Nations body of more than two thousand scientists researching climate change, gives the western U.S. a better than 90 percent chance of experiencing longer, hotter, and more frequent heat waves in this century. NOAA research meteorologist Martin Hoerling, an expert in climate dynamics, predicts that western droughts could last an average of twelve years, with some being worse than the 1930s Dust Bowl in the Midwest.

In October 2010, Aiguo Dai, a scientist with the National Center for Atmospheric Research, in Boulder, Colorado, announced stark findings: rising average temperatures will likely create increasingly dry conditions around much of the world in the next thirty years. By the end of the century, from the western United States to Asia, many regions will suffer droughts more severe than any others in modern times.

An internal Grand Canyon National Park report noted that average temperatures in the Southwest are expected to increase by about 6 degrees Fahrenheit (3.5 Celsius) by the end of this century, with summer temperatures increasing by nearly 8 degrees Fahrenheit (4 Celsius). Today's "extreme" temperatures that occur only every twenty years could occur every three years by 2050 and every other year by 2100.

Researchers have only begun examining what that will mean for ephemeral streams and springs critical to backpackers and for the plants and animals that rely on those scattered water sources. Some plants will migrate to higher, cooler elevations. Utah agave has moved up and down the canyon's walls for twenty thousand years. But others have gone as far as they can. The Grand Canyon rose, which called the Redwall Limestone home during the Pleistocene Epoch, now exists in just a few isolated populations on the canyon's uppermost layer, the Kaibab. This endemic flower may disappear for good from here.

Among the people I turned to for deeper answers was Ken Cole, a research professor with Northern Arizona University and a former paleoecologist and climate scientist with the U.S. Geological Survey in Flagstaff. He has written about a period called the post–Younger Dryas, which occurred 11,700 years ago, at the onset of the Holocene, the epoch during which human civilization emerged. He sees that time as an analog for this century, because average temperatures in southwestern North America back then rose more than 7 degrees Fahrenheit in less than a century.

"I could see the current plant species distribution [in the canyon] moving up about two thousand feet within seventy to ninety years," he told me. Ponderosa pine "may do quite well." But some higher-elevation species that live only on the rims, like Engelmann and blue spruce on the North Rim and Douglas fir on both rims, "are not going to be there," Cole said.

Seeps and streams will flow for a shorter season and evaporate more quickly. Most climate models predict a slight decrease in precipitation in northern Arizona's future, "and that's really a problem, because even 5 or 10 percent less precipitation coupled with warming—that becomes very serious, it changes the character of the landscape to a very arid desert," Cole said.

One long-term forecast he made struck me most powerfully. He illustrated this point with the example of an eastern United States deciduous forest arising from an abandoned farm field—a succession that has occurred in many rural areas, from New Hampshire to the Southern Appalachians. In that wet climate, with abundant forest nearby to seed the field, a mature second-growth forest will replace the field within a century, leaving no trace of the farm save for moss-covered stone walls.

But scale that process up to an entire ecosystem, in a desert with no existing plants in the vicinity to provide seeds, and you have a very different story. The ecosystem does not recover within a century—not nearly. Following the post–Younger Dryas and two previous, comparable warming periods that Cole studied, the time it took for the Southwest to "equilibrate," or return to the species composition that existed before the warming period, ranged from 1,200 to 2,700 years.

"I think it's a fairly conservative statement to say that with the climate change we're facing over the next hundred years, it's going to take well over a thousand years for plant communities to equilibrate to that," Cole told me.

IT'S HARD TO LEAVE an oasis in the Grand Canyon.

On our third afternoon, I'm lying back on a sleeping pad, luxuriating in the cool shade of a boulder and scrawny bush, a refuge so undersized that my feet stick out into the blazing sun. Several steps down a steep embankment, a stream not more than ankle deep clatters over ledges. That steady drone, a desiccating wind banging down Lonetree Canyon, and some scrub brush and rocks surrounding my bed seclude me in a pocket of sensory isolation. After finding this spot, I couldn't hear or see Penny, Jeff, or Jasmine, who had staked out their own little refuges from the sun; or Nate and Alex, who, as soon as we reached this creek two hours ago, resumed their mission of damming every tributary in the Grand Canyon.

The book on the ground beside me didn't keep me awake for very long.

Nate now lies curled up against my side. He still enjoys doing that, and I recognize it as a finite and irreplaceable gift, so I linger over opening it each time it reappears. He found me after finally tiring of his hydro project and the sun; I'm sure Alex similarly homed in on Penny's islet of shade. Nate's telling me something about *Star Wars* or spaceships or maybe modern weaponry; I'm still too groggy to hold up my end of the conversation. Fatherhood has taught me the invaluable skill of nodding and muttering "wow" at appropriate lulls in a child's eager monologue, without having to mentally download much more than the feel of my kid under my arm.

Shade, a breeze, nice campsites nearby, the reassuring percussion of water, and a child with nothing better to do than lie down with his father—at this moment, these things sure seem like all I could ever need. Some oases are of the mind and heart.

I wonder what the Anasazi words were for "Why do I have to leave this place?"

We have to put a few more miles behind us today, in order to make tomorrow, our trip's last day, manageable for our kids. Nonetheless, tomorrow will probably be the hardest day my nine- and seven-year-old have ever hiked: eight miles and four thousand feet uphill, most of that on the relentless ascent of the South Kaibab Trail. In frigid blasts of wind, on the eve of a storm bringing fresh snow to the rims, Penny, Jeff, Jasmine, and I will alternately walk beside Nate and Alex, gently prodding them forward. Jeff, a history buff, will debate with Nate, who devours history books, the import of the Battle of Crecy, which took place in 1346 in northern France during the Hundred Years' War. We will scramble up a steep slab into a cave high up the South Kaibab, laughing at the echo of our voices, the kids beaming with the pure amazement of finding themselves in such a place.

The only negative words I'll hear from either of them will come around midafternoon. Seeing our destination a thousand feet above us, Alex will look up and ask me, "Is that the South Rim?" When I tell her yes, she'll respond with a thought that has surely occurred to many adults on the South Kaibab Trail: "It's too far."

Now, in our shady nook at Lonetree Canyon, I tell Nate we have to hike a couple more hours today and that the others are tired, so I'll need him to be a leader and encourage everyone. He promises to help out.

Between here and our hike's finish, we will find no water. We have to leave here carrying all the liquid nourishment six people will need for twenty-four hours and one big day's climb.

I fill a ten-liter bladder, plus my three one-liter bottles, and load that twenty-seven and a half pounds of water into my pack, which already holds almost thirty pounds of food and gear. Walking even a slight incline will push my heart's tachometer into its red zone. Jeff fills an eight-liter bladder and his bottles, Penny and Jasmine three or four bottles each. We refill Nate's and Alex's one-liter bladders. Then we start walking in soft late-afternoon sunlight, across sprawling gardens of prickly-pear cacti, four-foot-tall beavertail cacti, and boulders as large as trucks, my pack sloshing very slightly side to side with each step.

Teddy Roosevelt voiced a still-revolutionary notion when he stood at the Grand Canyon in 1903 and said, "Leave it as it is. The ages have been at work on it and man can only mar it." The United States had only seven national parks then and no National Park Service; our first park, Yellowstone, was younger than Roosevelt. The country still embraced the myth of America's infinite natural resources and our destiny to exploit them. Roosevelt's thoughts weren't original—people such as John Muir had preceded and inspired him. But they still ring with the courage of conviction, a sound rarely heard in politics over the cacophony of self-interest.

T. R. had no idea of modern society's capacity for marring what the ages have been at work on.

The Grand Canyon will always be spectacular, of course. Only its skin will change; just as it has witnessed the entire parade of life of Earth, the rock will outlast humanity. People will still snap photos from South Rim overlooks a short walk from their air-conditioned cars. But it's hard to imagine that a hotter, drier climate, with less water, won't affect the number of backpackers who toil through its labyrinths.

Sentimentality loves a story that comes full circle. I want Nate and Alex to each lie in a shady spot beside Lonetree Canyon someday, snuggling with their own young kids, and recall being there with Penny and me—to feel the years and generations connect like railroad ties across a familial continent. I want to believe that enough water will exist on this plateau three decades from now to grant them that opportunity. But there seems little hope for that.

We may get a mulligan on most of life's choices. But many moments we only get to live once.

Penny at Vernal Fall, on the Mist Trail, Yosemite National Park, California.

CHAPTER 2

HOW DOES THE WATER
GO UP THE MOUNTAIN?

JUNE 2010

In the last week of June, deep in the backcountry of Yosemite National Park, at nearly ten thousand feet above sea level in California's High Sierra, the two tiny Grant Lakes remain mostly entombed in ice. Two to three feet of dense snow blanket the ground. Ringed on three sides by close cliffs that soar hundreds of feet, the lakes exist in a refrigerator of shade and cold mountain air for most of the year.

But these days the post-solstice sun, intense at this elevation, thins the snow cover by a few inches a day. In a patch of ground melted bare, a streamlet trickles out of the snow. It flows almost noiselessly over waterlogged earth and slips into a creek, which bursts from the mouth of a tunnel formed by the water undercutting the snowpack.

Here, not far below its birthplace in the Grant Lakes, the creek offers no hint of its dramatic destiny; if it took a different course, it might have remained anonymous, like a lot of backcountry streams. But its portentous name—Yosemite Creek—derives not from where it begins, but from where it ends.

Across a mountainous area encompassing dozens of square miles, from the Grant Lakes to the western slopes of 10,850-foot Mount Hoffman to the smaller Boundary Hill, snow bakes in the June sunshine. Spring's warmth releases a sea of water into streams pouring down mountainsides. Some of this water gets absorbed by the forests of western white pine, mountain hemlock, and lodgepole pine, or by the blooming lupine, mountain penstemon, and paintbrush bursting to life in the meadows. Some soaks into the soil or settles temporarily into lakes.

Yosemite Creek owns the rest of that water. With each tributary it absorbs on its downhill ride, the creek swells. It drums louder against boulders and gathers momentum.

Near its journey's climax, Yosemite Creek has grown to a speeding train of foaming, white, liquid muscle, emitting a steady rumble that hikers can hear well before they see the water. It races through a series of drops into basins of polished rock resembling a waterslide—except that no waterslide churns violently enough to remove a person's limbs. And no slide ends like this one.

Some ten or more meandering miles from the Grant Lakes, Yosemite Creek suddenly takes flight.

It funnels through a tight notch at the brink of a granite cliff and explodes into the air. Water droplets that were snow yesterday disperse in their free fall over Upper Yosemite Falls. A silky white curtain comprised of almost equal parts air and water fans out as it plummets a sheer 1,430 feet. The curtain slams into the rocks at its base in what is arguably nature's finest demonstration of an unstoppable force meeting an immovable object. The collision launches much of the water skyward, a mushroom cloud of mist rising from a sort of unceasing atomic detonation, a nonstop pulse of thunderclaps under a clear blue sky.

WE HEAR THE DISTANT, pouring-sand drone of Upper Yosemite Falls long before it is visible. We've hiked more than a thousand feet uphill under a baking sun, in air more dead than disco, with cumulous clouds of dust rising from our footsteps to crunch in our teeth. At an overlook, we stop for a drink and a snack.

Before us, Yosemite Valley's half-mile-high granite walls frame a richly green forest that, from this height, more closely resembles a supermarket display of broccoli crowns than tall trees. We stand behind a steel railing installed to protect the multitudes of novice hikers from the seemingly obvious hazard of walking off a cliff. The ever-present traffic centipede inches forward far below.

I'm hoping the sight of Upper Yosemite Falls will buoy the flagging morale of our little troupe. But it's some distance away, and right now it seems that my plan to march my family nearly four miles and three thousand feet uphill to the top of the waterfall—and then, of course, come down—was perhaps overambitious.

Alex drops heavily onto a rock. "I'm tired and *really* hungry!" she blurts out. She then clinically observes, "I don't think this is going very well."

Our young Shakespearean actor, Nate, reminds me that, by waking him this morning, I violated the natural rhythm of his circadian clock. He flatly informs me that I am solely responsible for his near-complete spiritual and physical disintegration. "I can't help it," he says. "If you're going to wake me up that early, it's your fault if I complain."

My twelve-year-old nephew, Marco Garofalo, a compact, athletic electrical wire who was thrilled to travel from Massachusetts to join us here, shows no signs of tiring. But he rigidly maintains a minimum twenty-foot buffer between himself and that railing, and nervously watches Nate and Alex when they approach it. I wonder how he'll manage the more-extreme exposure ahead on this trail.

Also with us is my mom, Joanne, an active seventy-three-year-old. She has returned to Yosemite Valley to repeat hikes she and I shared fifteen summers ago this month, when we caught the park's world-famous waterfalls raging at a level rarely seen. Since she climbed her first New England mountain thirty years ago, we've hiked in many places together, among them the Tetons, the Grand Canyon, and the Presidential Range. But even my unflappable mother has already told me, "This feels a lot tougher than it did fifteen years ago."

Penny, who offers a fairly reliable litmus test for when my plans are falling into an uncontrollable tailspin, surveys the collective bad attitude and mutters to me, "I don't know about this."

We are in "The Valley," a place routinely capitalized as a proper noun to signify its stature above all other such geographic entities. We have come to hike to some of the most spectacular waterfalls on the continent at a time of year when mountain snowmelt fattens them up so much that they create something like an extremely localized rainstorm.

Unfortunately, events have not proceeded as I'd envisioned.

The most formidable challenge to visiting Yosemite Valley is simply gaining admission. I'd hoped to camp below the giant walls, giving the kids hours to play in woods and creeks. But the campsites had been booked solid for months, as had lodging. So the six of us wound up in one large motel room in Mariposa, a tiny, low-elevation tourist burg of cheap digs and greasy spoons a winding hour outside The Valley. When we rolled into town yesterday afternoon, the thermometer read 100 degrees Fahrenheit. Breathing offered all the pleasure of smoking an exhaust pipe.

Plus, I knew we'd have to race each morning to reach the park's Yosemite Valley entrance before 9:00 a.m. to beat the incoming flood of cars that often prompts the rangers to close that entrance by mid-morning.

But the kids were ecstatic about having a swimming pool; and truth be told, my mom was not terribly crushed over the lost opportunity to sleep on the ground. So we stocked the minifridge with beer and cranked the room's AC—which, with some imagination, sounded a little like camping near Yosemite Falls.

DESPITE HAVING CRUELLY WAKENED my family at seven o'clock this morning, it is noon by the time we drive to The Valley, negotiate the traffic, park in a dusty lot the size of the Caspian Sea, and ride a shuttle bus to the Upper Yosemite Falls Trailhead. We have begun this huge uphill climb during the day's hottest hours.

Now, watching my kids wilt at this overlook barely more than a third of the way to Upper Yosemite Falls, I'm wondering whether we'll make the top.

I've learned that hiking with kids is a bit like trying to predict the wind; things can seem to be in your favor, or not, and then abruptly reverse direction. I watch them for subtle hints of fatigue or hunger, such as a lagging pace. They lack an adult's self-awareness. They drink when I urge them, but not always enough. They'll complain one moment that hiking embodies the most inhumane form of "torture," and "this is the worst day of my life!" The next, they'll dash ahead, suddenly excited. They are imprecise barometers of their own physical condition.

So I read them like an ancient mariner searching the night sky, trying to anticipate their needs before trouble arises.

Parenthood is complicated like that.

My mom rises slowly to her feet and starts upward; the boys dart ahead of her, insistent on leading, and Alex hurries to keep up. The trail turns a corner, where a breeze stirs the air. Then Upper Yosemite Falls comes into view, a column of water falling through more than a quarter mile of air.

I ask Marco, Nate, and Alex, "What do you think of that?" But they only stare, saying nothing.

It's easy to be hypnotized by the complex liquid topography of Upper Yosemite Falls. At its apex, a thick, brilliantly white pillar drops perhaps a hundred feet and crashes onto a big ledge, sending a horizontal geyser ricocheting straight outward. This eruption breaks up into a broad curtain raining watery tracer bullets that arc downward. Strong gusts occasionally blow the curtain to the left, a pendulum swing in defiance of gravity. The waterfall blossoms in its earthward plunge, spreading ever wider, the curtain shredding like tissue paper.

Below the falls, the creek drops another 675 feet through the middle cascades, mostly hidden in a gorge. It then pours over 320-foot-tall Lower Yosemite Falls, which is visited by exponentially more people than the upper falls because it's just a short, flat walk from the road. Yosemite Falls drops a total of 2,425 feet, making it the sixth-highest in the world. The upper falls alone ranks among the world's twenty tallest.

While Nate and Marco scurry ahead, Alex continues gazing silently at the waterfall, her brow knitted in thought. Finally, she asks me, "How does the water go up the mountain?"

What a great question.

To the eyes of a seven-year-old, Upper Yosemite Falls appears to materialize inexplicably from the top of this 1,400-foot cliff. So I explain to Alex that up there, beyond sight, a lot of melting snow fills that creek with water. But I don't try to explain, yet, that Yosemite Creek, like many High Sierra streams, is ephemeral—this creek and waterfall dry up by July or August every summer. A rare heavy rain in autumn may temporarily resuscitate the creek. It alternately trickles and freezes through winter. But as spring liquefies the prodigious high-country snowpack, a rejuvenated Yosemite Creek bulks up again, building to a crescendo in May and June.

Nor can I figure out, at the moment, how to describe for her one certain outcome of a warming climate: less snow in Yosemite's future. Snowfall has declined measurably for decades in virtually all parts of the world that receive it. In the Sierra, as across the Mountain West, snow melts out and streams reach peak runoff two to four weeks earlier than a half century ago. The upshot is that this waterfall and every other one in Yosemite will reach peak runoff weeks or months earlier in the year by the time Alex is grown up. The profound effects of this seasonal shift in water flows will reverberate throughout ecosystems across the western United States, the region that's home to many of our big wilderness parks.

Seeing and hearing the upper falls, it's hard to believe it dries up every summer. I remember a late-summer day years ago, when I looked toward Yosemite Falls and it wasn't there. For an instant, I assumed I must have been looking in the wrong spot, but I wasn't. It threw my sense of place off balance because Yosemite Falls is the marker that defines that corner of The Valley. Its absence feels as conspicuous as the Manhattan skyline's gap after 9/11.

A creek drying up and a waterfall disappearing are metaphors for the spiritual blow the place suffers. People flock to Yosemite Falls in May and June to see the column of water free-falling off of this cliff, showering the forest and trail below in a mist magically raining from a blue sky. But once it turns off in summer, few hikers give that cliff more than an accidental glance.

Someday, many of us may find ourselves struggling with my seven-year-old's question about how water will get up that mountain.

"GOOD NEWS! IT'S MUCH cooler up here!"

Nate shouts this encouragement down to us as we enter the expansive reach of the mist from Upper Yosemite Falls. By some small miracle, we've managed to knock off half of the uphill slog. The view of Yosemite Valley receding below triggers an outbreak of summit fever. For all the negative consequences of overcrowding in this magnificent place, The Valley retains the power to lift fallen spirits.

Nate announces his intention to blitz the last 1,400 feet without stopping, whether we keep up or not. Marco is down with Nate's plan. They take off, cranking up through switchback after broiling switchback.

Once we're past the mist, the sun's heat again seems to pour onto us. Alex hangs on my arm, insisting she can't take another step. My daughter has the fat reserves of a grasshopper; I know what she needs.

We sit on a rock. I pull out an energy bar and give it to her. I say something to Penny, and then turn back to Alex just a couple of minutes after handing her the bar; it's gone, and she's not even chewing. Five minutes after we sat down, she pops up and chases after her brother and cousin, and I realize we're going to make it.

The kids, in fact, collect energy and inspiration the higher we climb. And my mom, the patient, indefatigable tortoise to these young hares, motors steadily upward. At the top, we tiptoe along a catwalk of steps blasted out of the cliff face to a broad ledge, with another railing, at the waterfall's brink—all of us, that is, except Marco. But despite his discomfort with the catwalk's exposure, Marco summons the courage to walk out to the beginning of it. There, he poses for a photo, beaming.

The rest of us stand at the railing beside the lip of the falls, peering over. The column of water plunges away so far that it distorts perception: though the falls expands in its drop, from here it appears to shrink down to a pinpoint.

I wonder what it looks like from up here with no creek exploding into the air, no raucous cacophony of stampeding water, no sound but the wind. It might evoke a promise extravagantly delivered but in time forgotten, filling the ears of a visitor with the ringing silence of disappointment. It's a promise that can be fulfilled only by tiny white flakes from the sky.

ON THE ENTIRE PLANET, probably nowhere else receives as much snow as the mountains that stand like a bulwark along America's West Coast. California's Sierra Nevada—including Yosemite and Sequoia-

Kings Canyon national parks—and the Cascade Range of Washington and Oregon catch the storms that drink heartily from the world's greatest incubator of weather, the 64 million square miles of the Pacific Ocean. In the Cascades and Sierra, at least three-fourths of annual precipitation falls between October and April. At higher elevations, it falls as snow, which has defined these places for thousands of years, literally sculpting the landscape and dictating the breadth of life that exists here.

The ski area at Mount Baker in Washington's North Cascades averages 650 inches of white stuff a year and holds the world record for snowfall in one winter: 1,140 inches—that's ninety-five feet—in 1998–1999. (The following summer, two friends and I skied Mounts Shuksan and Ruth in the North Cascades in late July, seeing snow depths typical of May.) The second-biggest winter total ever recorded also occurred in the Cascades: 1,122 inches (93.5 feet), at Paradise Ranger Station on Mount Rainier in 1971–1972.

That copious snowfall and northerly latitudes sustain more than seven hundred glaciers—60 percent of the total in the contiguous United States—in the North Cascades, the stretch of mountains between Snoqualmie Pass on Interstate 90 and the Canadian border. (Several weeks after this Yosemite visit, between August trips to Mount Rainier and the Olympic coast, described in later chapters, Penny and I will backpack with the kids to Hannegan Pass and Copper Ridge in Washington's North Cascades National Park. We want to show them mountains where endless rows of spires stand like picket fences above slopes smothered under snow and ice. Penny and I have climbed some of those spires and Mount Baker. We also carried the kids in packs day hiking to Cascade Pass when Nate was two and a half and Alex was five months.)

In California's Sierra, it is not uncommon for a storm to dump six feet or more of snow. The U.S. Forest Service Sierra Snow Laboratory has recorded fifteen storms that deposited roughly ten feet or more. The biggest, from March 27 to April 8, 1982, buried the area under more than fifteen feet of powder, including sixty-five inches in twenty-four hours at Twin Lakes, just north of Yosemite. Mount Shasta Ski Bowl in Northern California—actually at the southern end of the Cascade

Range—is famous for setting a record that stood for years for the highest single-storm snowfall total: 189 inches, or nearly sixteen feet, over one week in February 1959.

Big snow years still occur. The winter of 2010–11 hammered the Sierra and the Cascades, with more than fifty feet of snow at Lake Tahoe's ski resorts and more than seventy-one feet at Mount Baker's ski area. But viewed from a longer perspective, in the words of Yosemite National Park hydrologist Jim Roche: "Snow is . . . an endangered resource."

Climate models offer different prognoses for the future of snow, depending largely on what steps society takes in coming years to reduce carbon dioxide emissions. Unfortunately, humanity has steadily emitted more CO_2 than even the worst-case scenarios in forecasts from the IPCC. Predicting outcomes for species gets difficult because of the myriad complex interactions of plants and animals, habitat and topography. But the behavior of water is extremely reliable: it freezes at 32 degrees Fahrenheit, or 0 degrees Celsius, and melts above it. Always has, always will.

Cascades snowpack has already declined by 15 to 30 percent over the past seventy years. Virtually all glaciers in the North Cascades, locus of the most extensive glacier research in the world, are in retreat, according to scientists with the North Cascades Glacier Climate Project and North Cascades National Park.

That ice currently holds as much water as all of Washington's lakes, rivers, and reservoirs combined. It provides a buffer against droughts and, in a region that is famously rainy but has dry summers, supplies one-fourth of the summer water supply, according to the North Cascades Glacier Climate Project.

The Skagit River, which produces more runoff than any Washington river except the Columbia, is one of the few Lower 48 watersheds that host all five Pacific salmon species: chinook (or king), chum, coho, pink, and sockeye. A diminished Skagit will actually alter Puget Sound's balance of fresh- and saltwater, with unknown repercussions for aquatic life.

Seven hydroelectric dams on North Cascades rivers supply electricity to the region, including one-fourth of Seattle's. Those dams also irrigate the Columbia Valley, which, despite a desertlike eight inches of annual rainfall, is home to much of the state's U.S.-leading $1.7 billion apple industry and its wine industry, which ranks behind only California's.

Philip Mote, now director of the Oregon Climate Change Research Institute at Oregon State University, predicted back in 1995 that it is "likely that the losses in snowpack observed to date will continue and even accelerate," especially in already mild, middle-elevation ranges like the northern Sierra and Cascades. Mote added that this decline, "already well under way, will have profound consequences for water use in a region already contending with the clash between rising demands and increasing allocations of water for endangered fish and wildlife."

Fifty-three North Cascades glaciers disappeared between 1971 and 2006. Glaciated area has shrunk 40 percent since 1850, and 13 percent just since 1971. By the time Alex and Nate are my age, researchers expect 70 percent of the glaciers, which have existed for perhaps sixteen thousand years, to be gone.

On our second morning in The Valley, as on most summer mornings, two of the most powerful currents in America churn side by side at the eastern end of Yosemite Valley, just a few miles from Yosemite Falls. One flows downhill and one uphill.

The gravity-driven torrent belongs to the Merced River, which is born in snow at up to thirteen thousand feet in Yosemite's mountains. From the air, the upper Merced suggests an enormous luge track. It drops eight thousand feet within just twenty-four miles—a plunge eight times greater than that of the Colorado River through the Grand Canyon, compressed into less than one-tenth of the distance. Two drops are dead vertical: 594 feet over Nevada Fall and 317 feet over Vernal Fall.

The uphill flow paralleling the Merced isn't some gravity-defying liquid. It's human.

The six of us wade into that river of hikers, weaving around jams of slower people on the most popular footpath in the park and undoubtedly one of the busiest in America: the Mist Trail. As if in a crowded shopping mall, I occasionally lose sight of the kids in the roiling sea of shuffling humanity.

I'm not worried about today's plan to hike up the Mist Trail to Vernal Fall and Nevada Fall. It involves about a mile and a half less distance and one-third less climbing than yesterday's trek. Everybody's well rested. Plus, I have the ultimate motivator stashed in my pack: a few pounds of chocolate.

On another warm, sunny June morning fifteen years ago, my mom and I panted up this steep trail together on our way to camp in the backcountry and hike Half Dome. We wore T-shirts and shorts, so it puzzled us that the scores of hikers coming down wore rain jackets—and they were all soaked, their hair matted, wet clothing pressed against their bodies. From previous visits, I remembered mist created by Vernal Falls as steady but not drenching. I just shrugged at my mom.

Then we rounded a bend and stepped into a downpour falling incongruously from a cloudless sky. We pulled on jackets, cinched the hoods tight, and walked bent forward into the monsoon sprung from Vernal Fall pounding the rocks at its base. That visit had coincided with peak runoff from rapid snowmelt in the mountains. The Merced bellowed like a pride of hungry lions that day.

Today, the Mist Trail remains truer to its name, showering but not blasting us. Energized by this bizarre phenomenon of rain materializing from sunshine, Marco, Alex, and Nate scamper up the steep trail's large granite blocks. I hustle to stay on their heels; Penny and my mom follow behind. The angle of sunlight through the mist launches a rainbow arcing down-canyon from the foot of the waterfall. At one point, Nate turns to me, his face creased in a grin, and gushes, "I can see why they call this the Mist Trail!"

The upper Merced drains a corner of the national park covering about 182 square miles—roughly equal to 140 Central Parks. A constellation of more than a thousand lakes helps sustain the river throughout summer, though its sound and fury diminish greatly by August.

The young river courses through a canyon of smooth granite walls carved by a glacier that, in the last ice age, was almost a mile and a half thick and extended twenty-five miles downstream beyond Yosemite Valley—the same glacier that sculpted the three-thousand-foot face of El Capitan. While exploring high in the mountains in 1871, the conservationist John Muir came upon the withered remnant of that mighty river of ice, and in doing so made the first-known discovery of a glacier in the Sierra Nevada. It disappeared in the 1970s. Vernal and Nevada falls probably lost some of their late-summer oomph after that, because that's a time of year when rain and mountain snows grow scarce, and melting glacial ice provides a last reserve for streams.

Below the waterfalls, the river hardly catches its breath, charging through a nearly unbroken cataract choked with boulders, some as large as boxcars. Over the eons, those granite blocks have sporadically detached without warning from the thousand-foot-tall cliffs overhead, raining hell onto this tight canyon—a frightfully destructive natural event that occurs with some regularity in The Valley, as well. In one incident in March 1987, an estimated 1.5 million tons of granite—like one-quarter of the Great Pyramid of Cheops suddenly crashing to the ground—fell off the cliffs named Three Brothers, closing Northside Drive for several months.

Above Vernal Fall, the kids stand at a railing near the brink. Shouting to one another over the deafening water, they take turns hurling sticks into the current, belly-laughing with approval as each gets swept over the lip. Penny, my mom, and I recline on sun-warmed granite slabs just a few steps from where, fifteen years ago, my mother and I laughed and dried out and never imagined that getting drenched by mist from Vernal Fall on a warm June day might someday cease to be possible.

RESEARCHERS FROM THE UNIVERSITY of California–Berkeley reported in an October 2008 article in the journal *Science* that average minimum temperatures in Yosemite had leaped 6.7 degrees Fahrenheit in the past century, much of that just since 1970.

"It will rain instead of snow most of the time maybe as high as Tuolumne Meadows at eight thousand feet," Yosemite National Park geologist Greg Stock told me. This shift from snow to rain as the primary source of Yosemite's creeks means waterfalls will peak during maximum rainfall, rather than during the peak of snowmelt. In other words, these falls may roar in February or March instead of May or June.

Then Stock gave me his opinion about that, and I suspect a lot of people share it.

"One of the neat things about Yosemite is that waterfalls are peaking around the same time as wildflowers and other plants are getting triggers to bloom—the trigger being sunshine and warmth," he said. "But with warmer temperatures, the water won't be there come May or June."

Stock is the park's first staff geologist. He grew up in the foothills near Yosemite, falling in love with the Sierra at a young age. Now he may be on duty when the park's last two glaciers dry up. He's in the midst of a three-year study on the Lyell Glacier—as in Charles Lyell, the father of geology—and the nearby Maclure Glacier, the only two remaining in the park, to predict when they will be gone.

"I go up to the glaciers three or four times a year, and each time I think about what that place will be like when the glaciers are gone," he said to me. He pointed out that Muir's discovery of the first known glacier in the Sierra catalyzed our understanding of how landscapes like Yosemite Valley formed. "We are losing a resource in more than one way when these glaciers disappear."

I talked about Yosemite's waterfalls with Mike Dettinger, a research hydrologist with the U.S. Geological Survey in California. Not only will waterfalls peak weeks or months earlier, he told me, but they will dry up earlier and remain dead for longer each year.

Plants are dormant in winter. Summer is when living things and ecosystems need water—but summers will be hotter and drier.

Already, impacts are cascading over the natural world. Flowers bloom weeks earlier. Chaparral and oak are replacing low-elevation conifers. The oldest and largest trees across the West, within forests of all types, are dying at unusually rapid rates—including in Yosemite, home to the oldest known lodgepole pine tree in the United States, believed to have germinated in 1381.

Plants and animals are migrating to higher elevations. In their 2008 *Science* article, the University of California researchers found half of twenty-eight small-mammal species monitored in Yosemite living, on average, 1,500 feet higher than when the pioneering biologist Joseph Grinnell surveyed park habitats from 1914 to 1920. Pinon mice had relocated up to three thousand feet higher.

Some creatures will eventually have no higher to go and become regionally or completely extinct. One species facing that threat is the pika, a mouselike member of the rabbit family that lives in high, rocky areas and emits a loud warning chirp that, I can tell you, delights children. Hotter and drier conditions will claim others, possibly including the Sierra's mountain yellow-legged frogs, which are declining by 10 percent a year.

Steve Thompson, a wildlife biologist and branch chief of wildlife management at Yosemite National Park, told me: "We are just beginning to scratch the surface in research on the effects of climate change, with only anecdotal evidence, and a deep sense of dread.

"We've underestimated the speed and magnitude of the change year after year," Thompson said. "We have animals that are adapted to a certain climate regime, and it's changing much more rapidly than they can adapt."

I asked Mike Dettinger when he expects we will see the fallout of this climatic shift. His response stunned me.

By around 2030, Dettinger said, no computer models project winters that are cooler than today's average. In other words, within two decades—when my kids are in their late twenties—winter will no longer be the cold, snowy season most people alive today grew up knowing. That will mark a tipping point, after which, Dettinger said, "you see major changes in the snowpack."

"Our projections for the Sierra are that, under really optimistic conditions—climate-change scenarios that have as little warming as any projections being made—by 2050, you're looking at anywhere from thirty to fifty percent less snow on April 1," Dettinger said. "It's not that there's less precipitation, it's just that it's pretty much all run off during our winter instead of waiting until summer. That's a major change in the pattern and timing of snowmelt.

"It's a really frightening thing," he added. "Within about twenty years, the Sierra Nevada and Yosemite will be really quite a different place."

And here's a point worth repeating: that's the best-case scenario.

To a hiker approaching from below on the Mist Trail, Nevada Fall looks like a giant white whale bursting out of a straw.

Like Yosemite Creek in the instant before it achieves liftoff over Upper Yosemite Falls, the Merced River funnels into a narrow rock gorge just before it hits the brink of Nevada Fall, effectively pressing the current's accelerator pedal to the floor. A liquid avalanche, as purely ivory as the virgin snow of its origin, explodes from the cliff top to hurtle seven hundred feet onto rocks. From the rubble of water and stone, a thick mist rises and ambles downriver like a drunken ghost, shoved forward by the waterfall-generated breeze.

The trail leads us up onto the tableland that forms the waterfall's lip. Pine forest hugs granite riverbanks. The Merced strolls through here with uncharacteristic placidity, albeit briefly, as if steeling itself for its upcoming leap. Hikers lounge beside the river.

We wander onto ledges alongside Nevada's waterspout and stare, infinitely transfixed by the marriage of water and gravity, by its contradictory capacity for both violence and peacefulness. Again, the kids toss sticks off the wooden footbridge over the river, watching them disappear into the current speeding toward the abyss. Later, hiking down the John Muir Trail, we pass beneath a "weeping wall," where water percolating through the earth seeps from an overhanging rock wall as if conjured by magic. We walk beneath water dripping onto our heads, the kids laughing and making a game of it.

But you can't squeeze water from stone. It either emerges under its own power, or it doesn't.

It's tempting to invoke a metaphor about faucets turned off. But the image doesn't nearly do justice to the scale of this. Yosemite contains more than three thousand lakes and 1,700 miles of waterways. The entire High Sierra extends four hundred miles north to south and seventy miles across, spanning an area at least four times that of Yosemite.

These mountains are so unbelievably dappled with lakes that a map looks like someone shook a brush dripping with blue paint over it. Thousands of miles of waterways wind through them. It's hard to overstate the importance of the High Sierra snowpack: it sustains many forms of life, from lodgepole pine to lupine, and provides most of California's water supply, 80 percent of which goes to the state's nation-leading, $35 billion agriculture industry.

Given all that, you might think these mountain snows, like a giant bank or multinational insurance company, would be deemed too big to fail. Unfortunately, creeks and waterfalls do not have political clout. They only make noise until they don't.

Many rivers and creeks will dry up in the fast-approaching summers of the new climate regime; others will run markedly weaker once their tributaries fall silent. What this means for the trees along creeks, the birds, deer, fish, and myriad species that rely on that habitat, the animals that eat those deer and fish, no one fully knows. But any first-grader can tell you what happens when you stop watering a plant.

An entire mountain range hushed by the catastrophic ebb of its lifeblood seems like a vision of Armageddon.

Descending the John Muir Trail back to The Valley, the kids rush downhill not much slower, it seems, than the Merced. All three of them become lost in the giddiness that intoxicates children as a good day somersaults toward its end and they trade breathless recollections of it, speaking in elevated voices to be heard over the thunder of the river and one another.

Marco's all but skipping along; he'll announce in the car later, "I want to do this again!" Nate sprints and slides on his shoes over sandy, flat slabs as if on ice. My mom shows no sign of fatigue as she keeps pace with the boys, holding their rapt attention with her veteran-hiker tales of drenching waterfall spray and standing atop Half Dome. Alex contentedly becomes engrossed in a word game with Penny, though I can see my daughter is getting tired.

Nearing the end, she trips, scrapes a knee, cries a little. So she and I walk together the rest of the way, holding hands and playing our "number game." On a bet, she miraculously guesses the number in my head exactly, winning an ice cream once we're down.

A mile off to our left, Illilouette Fall drops 370 feet into a narrow gorge cleaved into one of Earth's hardest rocks. Beyond these cliffs, beyond sight, Yosemite's Clark and Cathedral ranges stretch sharply angled crowns two and a half miles into the stratosphere, in supplication to a sky long generous with its winter snows. Hawks float on thermals with an enviable prospect of a mountain range backboned and ribbed by granite standing to over fourteen thousand feet above the sea, some peaks devoid of vegetation, composed entirely of stone, like arrowheads leaning against the azure sky. Today, from that hawk's perspective, much of this scene remains blindingly white, buried under frozen water awaiting its release into a vast vascular system of streams and rivers.

A person carrying backpacking gear and food can walk for weeks here without glimpsing civilization, through three national parks and some twenty wilderness areas, along streams and cascades so numerous that many remain nameless. That person would have ample opportunity to admire the handiwork of water—ancient, frozen water that shaped this infinitude of cliffs and peaks, and the flowing water that revives the land each spring.

The Sierra Nevada, Yosemite—they are about the rocks, yes. And the rocks will always be there. But water will never go up the mountain.

Iceberg chunks on a black-sand beach in Johns Hopkins Inlet, Glacier Bay National Park, Alaska.

CHAPTER 3

THE DISTANT RUMBLE
OF WHITE THUNDER

JULY 2010

The two big, dark mounds of bear poop make no sound. They speak no words. But they communicate a persuasive argument that we consider camping somewhere else.

The three oval depressions in the beach sand, where the brown bears had lain down to sleep, bolster that argument, as do the paw prints stamped all over the ground, some longer than my rubber boots and twice as wide. The scat is fresh, the impressions of long claws still intact in the sand. These bruins bedded down here last night.

Looking up, I scan the steep, treeless slope above this remote wilderness beach near the mouth of Johns Hopkins Inlet, fifty-five miles up Glacier Bay in Southeast Alaska. I let my gaze roam over cliff bands and boulders, scrubby vegetation and gullies that offer a hundred nooks for a thousand-pound predator to hunker down out of sight, yet close enough to know we are here. I picture a brown bear letting its nose pick curiously through the upwelling of powerful scents rising from our pack of a dozen people. I imagine it kneading this information with its small brain, mulling over what to do about these strange creatures.

Everyone mills around on the wet beach, stretching stiff legs and backs after spending the past few hours shoehorned inside kayaks. Nate circles me like a satellite, my shark boy almost constantly in motion. He chatters excitedly about the scat and prints, pouring out his stream-ofconsciousness thoughts on how we could fortify this beachhead and use our pepper spray to fend off an ursine assault. Alex hovers nearby, quietly inspecting and contemplating this evidence of carnivores perhaps fifteen or twenty times her size.

I've read that bears will sometimes stalk people for hours, even a day or more, as if considering the sporting ethics of taking such easy prey. I wonder how far away these bears are right now.

Just minutes ago, as the two-person kayak that Alex and I are sharing nosed onto the beach, our lead guide, Sarah Rennick, walked over to me.

"We're thinking of camping here. There's just one problem," Sarah told me. "It's a bear highway."

I nodded, thinking, Yes, that's a problem. Although we just met yesterday, I can already see that, in Sarah, we have not only a skilled and sensitive guide, but also a master of understatement.

The brown bear. *Ursus arctos.* Alaska's version of the grizzly bear. Can grow to more than a thousand pounds on the rich, fish-based diet available along the coast. Can sprint across open ground—and virtually all the ground here is open—faster than Lance Armstrong can pedal a bicycle. Brown bears: among the top three concerns Penny and I had about sea kayaking and camping for five days here with the kids, and far more viscerally terrifying than the other two—the notoriously wet, cold weather and even the frigid sea, which could suck the life from an adult in fifteen minutes if a kayak capsized.

I've read too many accounts of encounters between brown or grizzly bears and people. They rarely go well for the people.

A calm discussion ensues. Sarah and her assistant guide, Dan Berk, lay out our options. We could camp here tonight, they assure us. Bears are highly unlikely to approach so many people—statistically true, I know, but what do bears know about statistics? Of course, if they return, we might have to abruptly get into the kayaks and leave, maybe abandoning camping gear, possibly during the night. Everyone, no doubt, can envision worse scenarios, but no one goes there. Alternatively, the next prospective campsite is a thirty-minute paddle from here.

I hardly have to glance in Penny's direction to know she would no sooner camp here—with our kids—than in the bears' den. But for the rest, she firmly suggests, "I say we move on to the next campsite." My wife hardly expects me to agree with her on everything, but with this vote, I know which way I should cast my ballot to preserve marital harmony. It's midafternoon, overcast but not raining, cool but not freezing. Everyone's warm enough in our multiple layers of long underwear, fleece, rain slickers, hats, and neoprene gloves. No one's tired. We reach a remarkably speedy consensus to move on, the sense of relief palpable as we shove off.

Back in the kayak, I ask Alex what she thinks of leaving, and she says, "Well, I wasn't worried about it until I saw those big bear paw prints." That's my sensible daughter. Nate, on the other hand, might like to see us deploy our pepper spray on a bear. To him, weapons are like wings on a bird: no point having them unless you let 'em fly.

It's the second afternoon of our five-day sea kayaking trip run by Alaska Mountain Guides. With two guides and six other clients, we've come to paddle around Glacier Bay's upper West Arm, probing deep within a national park the size of Connecticut. And the park comprises just one-tenth of one of the world's largest and most pristine wildernesses, a UNESCO World Heritage Site sprawling over fifty thousand square miles—the size of Greece. We're here to see the original complement of North America's land and sea creatures, and towering mountains buried under snow and ice.

Most of all, although my kids do not yet grasp this, we've come to witness the last hurrah of the ice age. While conventional thinking has it that Earth's most recent glacial period ended ten thousand years ago, in Glacier Bay, you can watch its final act.

YOU COULD SAY THAT Glacier Bay has the most mobile ice on Earth. Nowhere else has seen so much ice migrate so far.

Two and a half centuries ago, the bay did not exist; it lay beneath one solid river of ice four thousand feet thick, up to twenty miles wide, and a hundred miles long, sticking its blue and white tongue out into Icy Strait. In 1794, when British Captain George Vancouver sailed HMS *Discovery* through Icy Strait past the bay's barely open mouth, he wrote in his ship's log of seeing a "sheet of ice as far as the eye can see." By the time John Muir arrived in 1879 to explore the bay with native Tlingit guides, the tongue of ice had pulled back more than thirty miles. At night, Muir wrote, "the surge from discharging icebergs churned the water into silver fire."

Today, this fjord extends sixty-five miles into the mountains. The glacier's withdrawal has uncovered an aquatic catacomb of channels and inlets with twelve hundred miles of winding shoreline—nearly as much coastline as Florida.

In Glacier Bay, nothing remains stationary, not for long. The glaciers surge down out of the mountains at average speeds of up to fifteen feet per day. Roaring with an explosive sound that the Tlingits call "white thunder," several glaciers frequently discharge massive blocks into the bay, at times choking their inlets with icebergs. The tide rushes in and back out again, a little boy unsure where he wants to play. Shifting as much as twenty-five feet, one of the world's greatest tidal extremes transforms vast mudflats to sea and back to mudflats twice every day.

Even the Earth's crust gets no sleep here. Relieved of the unimaginable weight of ice that had entombed it for much of the past 115,000 years, the land rises two inches a year, a rate unmatched anywhere else in modern history. Since the mid-eighteenth century, this process, called glacial isostatic rebound, has uplifted parts of Glacier Bay eighteen feet—constantly remaking the shoreline, knitting islands to the mainland, changing the flow of streams, remodeling the ecosystem, even increasing the rate of seismic activity in one of the more tectonically unstable parts of the world.

The glacier's retreat opened a window onto the past, replicating the North America of ten thousand years ago.

Glacier Bay displays a living time line of plant succession in the wake of deglaciation. In the lower bay, ice-free for 250 years, a mature temperate rain forest of spruce and hemlock grows almost impenetrably thick, watered by six feet of rain a year. Farther up the bay, the forest gets younger, dominated by deciduous cottonwood, willows, and alder. In the upper bay, where bare sea cliffs show the scars left by clawing glaciers that drew back within the past century, the landscape remains mostly barren. The thin soil sprouts only a few hardy shrubs and flowers, like broad-leaved willowherb, fireweed, and dryas, an early pioneer of northern Europe and North America ten millennia ago.

Closest to the active glaciers, you find only tundra. Just sixty miles from an old-growth forest, spores fly on the wind, birds transport seeds, and bare rock sprouts a nappy algal fur called "black crust." Life rises from the Earth's ravaged skin on the slimmest promise of existence.

This ongoing process of creation has birthed a sort of northern paradise. Humpback whales, orcas, and harbor seals ply the waters. Four of the five species of salmon native to the West Coast spawn here. Brown bears overturn stones on the beach in search of shellfish. Mountain goats scramble nimbly up sea cliffs. Sea otters pop furry heads above the water. Scores of Steller sea lions, the largest males ten feet long and weighing more than two thousand pounds, pile up in a mountain of angrily honking blubber on the barren rock of South Marble Island, where researchers have counted 1,100 of them.

A multitude of birds thrive on the fish-rich waters. Southeast Alaska sits along a major migratory flyway used by more than three hundred species of birds. We spot the pigeon guillemot with its red legs and beak; black-legged kittiwakes nesting in sea cliffs; pelagic cormorants diving 150 feet underwater for fish; and the rare horned puffin and more-common tufted puffin, which catch up to two dozen fish in their expansive bills to haul back to their chicks. Some species threatened or endangered outside Alaska, like the bald eagle and marbled murrelet, abound in Glacier Bay.

Our movements out here are just a sigh in the long, slow respiration of this place. In its rawness, Glacier Bay strips away the ornate vestments civilization tends to wrap around our lives. It reveals life as tenuous, and yet driven powerfully by the sole purpose of living.

Black crust, dryas, and spruce trees growing. Steller sea lions braying at one another in a cacophony that bears a striking resemblance to the playground at my children's elementary school. Penny and me exercising caution in choosing where we pitch the tents that our kids will sleep in. Nate and Alex collecting shells on the beach on their long, circuitous voyage to becoming whole adults with a world perspective partly formed by picking up shells on a wilderness beach below thundering glaciers. Or all of us exulting in dipping a paddle in the water here—these are just different manifestations of the same mission. We live only to live. It's no more complex than that. Sometimes we just need to be reminded of it.

FROM THE WINDOW OF a small plane cruising 1,500 feet above the mountains and sea, Southeast Alaska conjures an M.C. Escher drawing in which images of fish morph into birds. In this collage of water and earth, it's hard to distinguish a clear border between the two. Islands dapple the sea; lakes speckle the land. Fingers of ocean and continent poke one another endlessly.

The day before our brief visit to what I may always remember as Brown Bear Beach, Penny, the kids, and I sat inside a six-seat, twin-engine, oversized paper-towel tube with wings. Alex and Nate had eyed the small plane as if we were boarding a lawn chair rigged with balloons—Alex skeptical, Nate excited. With conversation stifled by the bawling engines, we gazed silently through rain-streaked windows at a rumpled land of steep hills covered by a shaggy green blanket. After bouncing onto the airstrip in the dirt-road town of Gustavus, on the outskirts of Glacier Bay National Park, we rode the park tour boat up the bay on a journey back in time.

The boat deposited us like banished pirates on Ptarmigan Beach, beneath leaden skies in the bay's upper West Arm. Our kayak armada followed the shoreline southeast to two-mile-long Reid Inlet, where we walked up to the hundred-foot-tall, severely cracked face of the Reid Glacier. A river of gray water burst from the garage-size mouth of a blue-ice cave in the glacier's snout.

In the evening, we sat around eating halibut burritos and drinking hot cocoa as clouds of tiny, biting insects called "white socks" violated our eyes, ears, noses, eyelids. Sarah said she had never seen a worse plague of them. Nate and Alex wore our two head nets. The next morning, as we packed up gear in more insect clouds, Nate would say to me, "Okay, let's find a less buggy place to camp tonight."

Around 9:30 p.m., after everyone had retired to their tents, I stood outside in the long sub-Arctic dusk drinking up the view across the inlet's glassy water to the Reid Glacier—much of it streaked with dirt, other parts the clean blue of the midmorning sky, of time expressed in frozen, compressed water molecules. In his lovely book *The Only Kayak,* about living in Glacier Bay, Kim Heacox describes a 1979 kayaking trip when icebergs from the Reid Glacier filled this inlet. Three decades later, with the glacier almost entirely receded onto land, no bergs floated within my view.

SILENCE SUMMONS OUR ATTENTION more insistently than noise. Living in civilization corrupts the senses like that. My kids, thankfully, know the steady tone of quiet, a sound many children today would not recognize.

I rest my paddle across the kayak, letting the boat drift. The water of Johns Hopkins Inlet lies flat and still. There's no wind, just some barely audible hum in the distance, a few decibels cut adrift from a howl high in the mountains. The soft drone of a waterfall a mile or two behind us fades to a whisper as we move farther from it, then snuffs out. A bald eagle screech pierces the quietude briefly, but is suddenly gone, like a stone dropped into a pond. The silence feels dense enough to float atop on our backs, arms outstretched, eyes closed.

Late on our second afternoon in Glacier Bay, thirty minutes past Brown Bear Beach, we approach another beach of stones where we'll spend two nights. We're alone out here, no other boats or people in sight. Alex and I trail a couple of hundred yards behind the group, our kayak weighed down by gear and food for five days and powered by a single engine: me. Penny and Nate, in a smaller, lighter, two-person kayak, keep up with the others.

I hadn't expected my seven-year-old to really contribute to our propulsion, of course; and it matters not, because our companions are in no hurry. Alex keeps promising to help me paddle, just as soon as the feeling moves her. She's been saying this for two days, and it cracks her up every time.

We look up at a bald eagle in its nest atop a snag high up a nearby sea cliff. "He's watching the kayakers go by," Alex explains to me.

Marbled murrelets dive for fish. A harbor seal pokes its slicked head above water not fifty feet away, investigating us with dark eyes. I hear Alex faintly catch her breath as she and the seal exchange stares for an instant, before it disappears with a *bloop*.

Then a sharp concussion, like a large-caliber gunshot, rips the quiet open.

About six miles away, but visible to us at the other end of the inlet because it's so massive, the mile-wide, twelve-mile-long Johns Hopkins Glacier has spontaneously cleaved off another immense piece of itself with a booming detonation.

The Hopkins Glacier is the most active remnant of the river of ice that once filled Glacier Bay. Today, four other so-called tidewater glaciers still extend from the mountains to the sea in various inlets, Bruce Molnia tells me.

A research geologist with the U.S. Geological Survey who's been studying Alaskan glaciers for more than forty years, Molnia first saw this bay in the 1970s, when twelve glaciers reached tidewater. His favorite place to kayak was Muir Inlet, where the Muir Glacier, like the Hopkins today, regularly spewed icebergs into the sea. More than a thousand seals hauled out on those bergs to birth pups every May and June and nurse them for several weeks, safe from the brown bears and orcas. Birds filled the sky, living well on the fish attracted to the nutrient-rich waters churned up by the active ice.

In 1993, the Muir Glacier crawled up onto land like a stranded sea creature taking its last breaths. Today's it's a "wasting glacier," its terminus blanketed in dirt and rocks, melting in place. When the bergs left Muir Inlet, the seals followed, as did the orcas, many of the birds, and the kayakers.

Over the past sixty years, Alaska's average temperature has increased 3 degrees Fahrenheit, three times the worldwide rate. Winter and spring temperatures are rising even faster. The winter mean in Juneau, near Glacier Bay, has risen almost 7 degrees. Molnia reports that more than 99 percent of Alaska's glaciers are retreating. Many that reached tidewater for centuries do so no longer.

While average temperature year-round dictates whether mountain glaciers grow or shrink, tidewater glaciers exhibit more complex dynamics because they terminate underwater, according to professor Tad Pfeffer of the Institute of Arctic and Alpine Research (INSTAAR) at the University of Colorado–Boulder. Pfeffer has studied the last of Alaska's large tidewater glaciers to begin retreating, the Columbia. It has withdrawn more than ten miles since 1982—despite flowing an average of more than sixty feet per day, making it, at times, the world's fastest glacier. Like a runner on a long, speeding treadmill, the Columbia reels backward even faster than it sprints forward, dumping a cubic mile of ice a year into Prince William Sound.

As the climate warms, a tidewater glacier thins and spreads out, allowing it to flow more rapidly along its bed. This speeds up its calving, creating a positive-feedback mechanism that accelerates until the glacier has run aground. In other words, once warming pulls the plug, a tidewater glacier's demise is just a matter of time. "This is triggered by climate, but once it starts, it will continue almost regardless of what climate does," Pfeffer told me.

The sky clears, revealing tall, razor-edged mountains with sheer walls and great coats of snow and ice. Tendrils of cloud wrap like scarves around pointed summits. The highest, Mount Fairweather, scrapes the sky at 15,325 feet just twelve miles from the Pacific Ocean. Icebergs float in the bay, some as large as a car. Where the shoreline is not cliffs rising straight out of the water, the land is composed of stones and scattered, scraggly bushes, a few flowers lending a patch of color, and nothing else.

Captain Cook saw these peaks in 1778, during an identical short reprieve from the typically wet, gray Southeast Alaska weather, and named them the Fairweather Mountains. It may be the most misleading place name on the planet. But that's what happens with the sun comes out here: it's the opiate of Southeast Alaska. You can't help but feel optimistic.

That solar-powered optimism recharges all of us at our new campsite, surrounded by icy mountains reflected in Johns Hopkins Inlet. The few mosquitoes seem like a precious gift compared with our last camp. Every ten or twenty minutes, another peal of white thunder rolls out of the blue sky.

We're becoming fast friends with our kayaking teammates. Megan and Jules, two young women from Perth, Australia, are out here on a short "break" from a months-long bicycle odyssey from Alaska to Central America. Chris, an engaging, fiftysomething nutritionist at Penn State University, is here with her niece, Presley, a college student, aspiring doctor, and sometime nanny who quickly befriends Nate and Alex. Mike and Arlie, a young American couple living in Vancouver, British Columbia, talk to me about backpacking and skiing. Dan, in his early twenties, laughs off our kidding about his cigarette smoking and shares stories of guiding mountaineering trips and flying in small planes with daredevil Alaskan pilots determined to make him throw up.

Sarah—who admits to the nickname "Sarahdactyl," bestowed on her by girlfriends—has a gregarious, warm personality and a laugh that explodes from her throat. She breaks out her collapsible hula hoop and shows off her skills, spinning it up to her armpits and down around her ankles. Everyone takes a turn. Alex, who's tried it maybe once before, discovers her inner hula hooper. Long after everyone has had their fill, she stands off to one side practicing.

Three hours later, still at it, she complains with an "awwww" when Penny and I say it's time to hit the tents. But both kids pass out minutes after crawling into their bags and don't wake up for almost twelve hours.

Nights here are narcotic. I sleep as deeply as if it were my last sleep, and surprise myself by awakening three hours later than I do at home.

LIKE AN ICE-CREAM CONE in the warm sun, the cold regions of the world are melting fast—faster even than scientists or computer models have anticipated.

Greenland's ice cap, which stores enough freshwater to raise the world's sea level by twenty-three feet, is shrinking three times faster than ten years ago, according to a 2009 report by a group of international scientists. The Jakobshavn Glacier on Greenland's west coast, which holds more freshwater than any other single frozen feature in the Northern Hemisphere, retreated nearly six miles in the first decade of this century.

Arctic Ocean sea ice coverage reached record minimums in 2002,

2005, and 2007, when its area was 39.2 percent below the 1979–2000 average. And 2010 marked the fourteenth straight year of below-average sea ice extent. Sea ice reflects sunlight, insulating the Arctic, whereas open ocean absorbs solar heat. As sea ice wanes, a positive-feedback loop ensues—the ocean absorbing more heat, melting more sea ice, allowing the ocean to absorb yet more heat.

Scientists no longer debate whether the Arctic Ocean will become entirely ice-free in summertime in coming years, only when it will happen.

As the permafrost that has locked up one quarter of Northern Hemisphere lands for twelve thousand years steadily thaws, it releases tremendous volumes of methane, which warms the atmosphere twenty times faster than carbon dioxide. This spawns yet another positive-feedback loop, the air warming faster as more methane escapes, melting even more permafrost.

The Arctic acts as a driver of world climate, influencing even the Gulf Stream, which keeps much of northern Europe warmer than other land masses at comparable latitudes. The Arctic is the breeding ground and marine breadbasket for vast numbers of mammals, birds, fish—and humans. As one National Oceanic and Atmospheric Administration scientist put it, "Whatever is going to happen in the rest of the world happens first, and to the greatest extent, in the Arctic."

At the bottom of the Earth, average temperatures on the 900-mile-long Antarctic Peninsula have increased by 5 degrees Fahrenheit in sixty years—and winter temperatures by 11 degrees. Sea ice now covers the Southern Ocean off the Antarctic Peninsula for three fewer months a year than it did in 1979. For three decades, dozens of studies have warned of the potential for the West Antarctica ice sheet to melt, releasing 4 billion cubic yards of freshwater and raising global sea level by sixteen feet.

Massive coastal ice shelves are breaking up, some as large as small U.S. states—a phenomenon that Ohio State University geologist John H. Mercer had anticipated way back in 1978, in an article in the journal *Nature*. His forecast was predicated on the rate of fossil-fuel consumption continuing; but of course, the rate has multiplied since 1978.

Mercer's calculations were off in just one important aspect: he thought Antarctica's ice shelves would not begin disintegrating for another twenty years.

"Dad!"

Nate hurls my whispered name across the beach like a well-aimed snowball. Hearing my son whisper is a rare enough phenomenon for me to turn my head. So when he holds a finger over his lips and beckons for me to follow, the hook is set. I put aside my breakfast of eggs, sausage, and hash browns and tiptoe with him very slowly toward the water.

He stops and points. At the water's edge, two birds about the size of ravens, with long, pointed, red-orange beaks, poke around in the tide-greased rocks. Oystercatchers, they step stealthily, giving us wary glances. We watch them in silence from about twenty feet away for several minutes. But the encounter sears an impression of greater longevity: days and weeks later, Nate will remind me how he showed me those birds. I suspect he'll remind me years from now.

The sky glows an iridescent blue. The bay could pass for a clean pane of glass if not for the occasional slight ripples dashing across it. The sun's warmth penetrates our long-sleeve thermal jerseys—the lightest we've dressed in three days—as we wriggle into the kayaks and dip paddles into the flat water, pointed up the inlet to visit the source of those frequent claps of white thunder.

Gray waterfalls pour over cliffs, fed by high fields of snow and ice. We weave among hundreds of floating and bobbing bergs, wildly sculpted by wind and waves. Alex points to one that looks like a swan, to another like an arch. Some are blue, others carry dirt and dark stripes, possibly calved from the underwater portion of the glacier—ice missiles that can surface without warning and flip a kayak. The Hopkins Glacier bellows with each calving, as if warning us to stay away. Its frigid breath reddens our cheeks.

In the kayaks, we sit at water level, an inch of plastic separating us from the icy abyss. We are like amphibious centaurs—partly submerged but breathing air, ostensibly the most intelligent creatures out here, but arguably the least well-adapted, the most self-destructive. Alex reaches out and touches a passing softball of compacted snowflakes from three centuries ago.

Just as we all paddle past one couch-size berg, it begins popping and sizzling, releasing bubbles of ancient air. It rocks, growling like an agitated animal—then abruptly implodes, collapsing in on itself, disintegrating into a floating blob of slush. Witnessing their first "bergie seltzer," as it's known, Alex and Nate erupt in laughter, filing away another anecdote for recounting later. I add this mental image of a berg rolling to the litany of hazards out here.

A little while later, I notice Alex slowly listing to starboard, and finally realize she has fallen asleep, lulled by the warm sun and gentle rhythm of the boat quietly cutting through the water. When she sits upright again after about forty minutes, I ask her, "How was your nap?" She smiles over her shoulder, pauses, and then tells me, "I like kayaking trips because you can take a nap while your partner's paddling."

Three hours from camp, we weave more deliberately through an increasingly denser archipelago of bergs—the biggest, freshly calved ones like white islets. Then we swing toward shore. Nearly a mile away still, the Johns Hopkins Glacier rises a sheer 250 feet out of the water and stretches a mile across, spanning the inlet from cliff wall to cliff wall like a colossal white dam. Its size defies visual comprehension in a landscape without scale cues such as trees, where cliffs scratched down to polished rock burst from the sea.

Each explosive calving calls to mind a mortar strike against a tall building—a poof of white dust, a bus-size chunk of wall falling away, smashing into the water. The glacier's cracked white tongue, streaked with dirt and rock scraped off the mountains, undulates backward farther than our eyes can follow, splitting into roots buried deeply into pyramidal peaks.

We drag the kayaks onto a black-sand beach. Irregularly shaped baseballs and basketballs of blue and white ice litter the immaculate ebony grains, the contrast hypnotic in an environment without vegetation, impoverished of color. A multi-tiered cascade of brown water roars over a cliff backing the beach, the foaming muddy torrent stampeding toward oblivion in the placid sea. "It's named Chocolate Falls," Dan says. Of course it is.

After three days spent mostly in sweaty, knee-high rubber boots, everyone yanks them off to luxuriate in the sensation of bare feet on sun-warmed black sand. Alex and Nate launch immediately into constructing a sand castle. Someone pulls out binoculars and we see that the scores of tightly packed bergs across the inlet are covered with hundreds, possibly thousands of seals.

Standing on the beach, Penny says to me, "Even on your list, this must be one of the most beautiful places you've ever been." Wild places I've visited in my work as a magazine writer flash to mind: numerous U.S. national parks, New Zealand's Fiordlands and Southern Alps, Iceland's Landmannalaugar area, Patagonia's Torres del Paine and Dientes de Navarino, the Swiss Alps, the Scottish Highlands, and the Himalaya.

She's right.

WHAT WILL BECOME OF Glacier Bay? When Nate and Alex are my age, the Johns Hopkins Glacier will probably still be calving into the sea, Bruce Molnia tells me. He thinks the park's four other tidewater glaciers are good for at least twenty years—but "beyond that, who knows? If you'd asked me thirty years ago what was going to happen to Muir [Glacier], I probably wouldn't have predicted it was going to become this wasting glacier."

Brendan Moynahan, who oversees the Park Service's long-term tracking of critical natural resources in Southeast Alaska, told me, "There will be big, unexpected changes. We know that things will get generally wetter and warmer. But for a place like Southeast Alaska, where the annual mean temperature is right about the freezing mark, a very small change in temperature one way or the other makes a big difference on the landscape—whether [precipitation] falls as rain or snow."

The fate of plants and animals appears hazier, but worrisome. Glacier Bay's harbor seal population, once one of Alaska's largest, has declined markedly since the early 1990s, on the order of 8 percent a year in Johns Hopkins Inlet and 12 percent annually at terrestrial sites around the bay, according to park wildlife biologist Jamie Womble. Steller sea lion numbers have dropped by half in recent years. The population of the rare Kittlitz's murrelet, a bird endemic to Alaska that nests and breeds in recently deglaciated areas of Glacier Bay, has plunged by 80 percent in thirty years. In each case, researchers are trying to answer why. Still, these examples of the relatively few species that have been studied hint at a broader trend probably mirrored in many species about which we know little.

But the biggest looming ecological disaster, not just for Glacier Bay but worldwide, may prove to be our undoing of the oceans, the birthplace and nursery of all life. While well-documented crises like overfishing, oil spills, and vast armadas of floating plastic trash are strangling sea life, the less-publicized acidification of the sea may ultimately eclipse all of those anthropogenic plagues. By absorbing about one-third of human-caused carbon dioxide emissions, the oceans have so far prevented even more warming. But our ocean parent is fast approaching its capacity for protecting us from our self-destructive tendencies. When salt water absorbs CO_2, it produces carbonic acid. Ocean surface water is now 30 percent more acidic than it had been in the past 25 million years, and is going through the fastest shift in chemistry since the time of dinosaurs, according to researchers in Britain's Ocean Acidification Research Programme. Britain's Royal Society calls this shift "essentially irreversible."

Researchers are only beginning to understand what that means for the web of life. But already, coral reefs are dying worldwide. Evidence strongly suggests that increasing acidity will harm shellfish and organisms at the bottom of the food chain, like krill, with devastating consequences for fish, seabirds, whales, sea lions, and many other species. One 2009 study found that a 10 percent decline in tiny, snail-like pteropods would cause a twenty percent drop in the body weight of pink salmon, a vital nutrient source for many animals, people, and the streams where they spawn and die.

The ocean's acidity could leap another 150 percent in this century. More immediately, the oceans may face a "tipping point" within two decades, after which life forms begin dying off rapidly, a team of scientists from the Australian Institute of Marine Science warned in a January 2009 article in *Science*. And Glacier Bay takes hits from many sides: cold water holds more carbon dioxide than warm water, so it acidifies faster. The freshwater entering from many streams reduces the seawater's ability to temper the effects of acidification, and melting glaciers only exacerbate that.

In a 2008 article, NOAA research scientist Sue Moore wrote, "The Arctic climate has changed demonstrably in the last fifty years, with further projected changes of a magnitude not seen during the time frame of human history." Many other experts talking about many other corners of the globe have echoed the ominous thought in the latter part of Moore's observation: " . . . not seen during the time frame of human history." What they're really saying is this: societies will be forced to adjust to a planet *that humans have never lived on.*

This makes bear poop on the beach seem like a relatively benign threat.

THE MISTING SLOWLY COALESCES into a light rain, then a steady shower. It's the kind of rain common from Southeast Alaska to the Pacific Northwest—not Atlantic-hurricane or New Zealand torrential, but more of a patient drowning. The distant shore and mountains across the bay's West Arm fade into fog. Oppressively dreary, dark gray sky and flat water pockmarked by raindrops bleed together on an indistinct horizon that could be two miles away, or two hundred yards. Our kayak convoy appears to float suspended, conspicuous dabs of color against this drab background.

There's no wind, but the wet, raw air cuts through our clothing layers into flesh, pouring ice water over bone. I keep paddling to generate body heat, but I can see that Nate, in the forward cockpit of my kayak for our fourth afternoon, has given up on paddling. He hunkers down inside his rain slicker and hood, arms crossed, chin in his chest, folding in on himself against the invasive chill. Alex sits similarly immobile in Penny's kayak. I worry that they are getting too cold, with a couple hours of paddling in this bleak rain to go before we reach our final campsite on Ptarmigan Beach.

Nate asks for my digital voice recorder, which I use to keep notes, and softly records observations that I won't hear until transcribing the files weeks later, at home. He describes a tremendous calving from the Lamplugh Glacier, another tidewater goliath we passed minutes earlier. Nearly a mile across, I imagine its shattered, 150-foot face of dangling seracs topped by razor turrets of ice looking to my kids like the castle of an evil witch. Nate also notes in my voice recorder that the park boat picks us up tomorrow, "and I'm looking forward to having a decent heater."

But then Penny and Alex pull up close by us and Alex says to me, laughing, "What, do you think it's raining?! It's sunny out!" As miserable as it is out here, I clearly don't have to worry about my daughter's spirits.

I wonder what Nate's thinking. "What are you going to tell your buddies at home about this trip?" I ask him.

From under his hood, without hesitation, he responds, "I think I'm going to need about a week to tell them all the stories from this trip."

My boy's words warm my chest like a hot drink.

We trace a shoreline of mossy cliffs where one waterfall after another—three, four hundred feet tall—flutters like a white ribbon. A bald eagle perches in a snag high up a cliff; Sarah points out its nest not far off, where its mate stretches wet wings. A porpoise surfaces and dives.

The final act of the ice age is an impressive performance. But the show is a mystery that leaves many questions unanswered, including how and when it will end.

Nate and Alex below Mount Rainier in the Spray Park area
of Mount Rainier National Park, Washington.

CHAPTER 4

IN THE LONG SHADOW
OF "THE MOUNTAIN"

AUGUST 2010

In the first week of August, summer has finally arrived in Washington's Mount Rainier National Park, a bit tardy but with much pomp. The Cascade Range has thrown off its thick blanket of snow from last winter and spring, erupting in a riot of photosynthesis. We plod uphill through relentless switchbacks in the shade of Pacific silver fir, Alaska yellow cedar, and other tall conifer trees. Spanish moss hangs in gossamer veils from branches. Thick moss carpets rocks. Ferns huddle together. With snowmelt and occasional rains swelling every river and stream, the forest is a happy drunk on an H_2O bender.

In the cool shade, with the temperature hovering around 65 degrees Fahrenheit and an energetic breeze wandering through the big trees, the weather seems copied and pasted directly from my backpacking dreams. I'm barely breaking a sweat despite carrying a pack weighing around sixty pounds—the approximate equivalent of my nine-year-old son riding me piggyback for several hours. (The pack, more forgiving than my son, does not ask me, "Can't you walk any *faster*?")

Hopefully, the payoff for this effort will be cultivating in Alex and Nate the desire that Penny and I share to return to the wilderness again and again. "Someday, I'll carry most of our stuff in my pack," Nate has eagerly promised me. I tell him, with more sincerity than he can possibly grasp, that I can't wait.

Joined by a Seattle-area hiking and climbing friend, Larry Gies, we're on the first afternoon of a three-day, twenty-four-mile backpacking trip across Rainier's northern flanks from Mowich Lake to Sunrise. As we hike, Penny and I volley Nate and Alex back and forth, taking turns playing one-on-one, engaging them in conversation to keep their minds off the miles. Periodically, we regroup to play "the story game," in which someone begins a made-up tale and we each in turn add to the plot. "The girl in the family can turn invisible," Alex says. "The boy can fly," Nate explains. Every story unfailingly culminates in a climactic battle—and laughter. Maybe the game will ultimately end with richer imaginations, enhanced abilities to envision a different narrative, to see another way. Imagination may be my kids' most useful tool in the world they will know as adults.

Alex and Nate are like those ferns, it occurs to me: young, supple, growing as if cell reproduction were a short-distance race. Like those ferns, with luck, my kids will get through childhood with nothing big falling on them, metaphorically speaking. I'm like one of those thicker, older trees—not so flexible anymore, less able to bend instead of break in a strong wind, wondering when a strong gale will knock me down.

Better not to dwell on that last point too much.

Beyond the narrow corridor of this footpath, the chaotic geometry of the temperate rainforest mimics a crowded city—without the traffic rodeo, noise, or bad air. The detritus of decades of trees toppling over lies strewn about in crosshatched piles; some lean precariously against those still standing. Rampant fecundity exists side by side with decay, giving the forest a complexity that is simultaneously beautiful and evocative of vast ruins.

Our surroundings stir up memories of the unimaginable devastation I saw while hiking in this park three summers ago, in the wake of record flooding. That episode was just the latest in a series of storms and floods in recent years that are redefining normal in this part of the country, alarming climatologists, park managers, and people living downstream of the Pacific Northwest's biggest mountain.

Meanwhile, I'm trying to not think about the forecast for rain over the next two days. Besides witnessing the aftermath of that record flooding, I have seen firsthand how fierce Pacific Northwest storms can get.

"THERE'S ABSOLUTELY NO ONE out here," I thought.

It was October 2003 and I was taking a solo, three-day hike around the park's Northern Loop. Even in the wilderness of many national parks, seeing absolutely no one for days—conjuring a sense of this country's wild edge before western settlement—is a rare gift. But for two clear, crisp autumn days I basked in complete solitude and jaw-unhinging views of Mount Rainier and its meadows. Then the rain came.

Throughout my second night, wind and water lashed at my shivering tent. In the morning, I set out in a downpour punctuated by windborne sheets of water that hit me as if hurled from a barrel. I crossed a slick log bridge over a creek so bloated that its white teeth gnashed at the ten-inch-wide platform beneath my boots. Had I gotten there an hour later, the bridge might have been gone.

I hurried the miles to my car, anxious to be dry—not fully aware of the urgency of escaping quickly. I did not know that this would become the second of three storms *within just eleven years* to cause 100-year or bigger floods in the Pacific Northwest. Or that the third tempest of that triad, in November 2006, would swell the Carbon River sufficiently to erase a huge swath of the trail I was hiking and the road I would drive out on.

Now I have returned to hike that same trail with my family.

WE EMERGE FROM THE forest, cross a log bridge over a stream, and step into a sunny meadow, where a vision of impossibility sits on the horizon. Mount Rainier stands implausibly tall and broad, a shaggy old bison of a mountain surrounded by coyote-scale peaks. It muscles into the sky, surreally massive.

With a summit 14,411 feet above the sea, Rainier rises anywhere from 8,000 to 11,000 feet above hikers on trails around its base—its visible relief is some two vertical miles. In "topographic prominence," a measure of a mountain's relative stature, Rainier ranks first in the contiguous United States, third on the continent, and twenty-first in the world. I remember feeling this same disbelief the first time, years ago, that I saw "The Mountain," as western Washington residents affectionately call it. It can make you wonder whether the delicate fruit that is your frontal lobe has spoiled badly in the hot subalpine sun.

We've entered Spray Park, a corner of Mount Rainier National Park popular with hikers. At about six thousand feet above sea level, these undulating meadows, which sprawl over an area comparable in size to Manhattan's Central Park, are renowned as one of the Pacific Northwest's best spots for wildflowers. Lupine, phlox, bear grass, pink monkeyflower, and others create a mosaic of deep-blue, yellow, white, pink, and purple against a backdrop of Rainier's blinding snow and ice.

Hoary marmots, chomping on plants just a few steps off the trail, pop their heads up and glare at us, making sure we have no interest in eating them, before returning to their meal. Nate and Alex watch them, fascinated, more interested in marmots than in wildflowers. "We have flowers at home," Nate reminds us.

Long ago, The Mountain's environs earned a fitting nickname also bestowed upon the ninety-three-mile-long trail that loops around Mount Rainier: "Wonderland."

Moving across Spray Park, we run into day hikers, many of whom stare at our kids and ask how old they are. It happens to us everywhere. As a culture, we set low expectations of children physically and of their relationship with the natural world.

But we have these wildflower meadows mostly to ourselves, as well as views of Rainier's steep north face. Like the north faces of mountains across the Northern Hemisphere, it receives limited direct sunlight, so it sustains The Mountain's biggest rivers of ice: the Carbon, Winthrop, and Emmons. While climbing the Emmons a few years ago, I looked out over Rainier's myriad pinnacled ridges of broken volcanic rock that probe outward like the arms of a starfish. But stand far away—say, forty miles away, in Seattle—and the fifth-highest peak in the Lower 48 can appear to float on clouds, immutable, eternal, a physical wonder.

In reality, it's almost as transitory as the seashore.

Mount Rainier is anything but stable, a truth that humans have probably recognized since our ancestors first set foot on its slopes seven thousand years ago. All mountains crumble to the sea, of course. But glaciated stratovolcanoes like Rainier are in the accelerated program. The forces shaping Mount Rainier are a vehicle with four gears. First gear idles deep within the Earth's crust, bringing change at the slowest speed, across spans of time unfathomable to us. Rainier sits within the Cascade Arc, a chain of fifteen or more volcanoes straddling a fault line stretching from Northern California to southwestern British Columbia. Created by the subduction of the Juan de Fuca, Explorer, and Gorda plates of the Earth's crust underneath the North American Plate, this process built up the cone of Rainier half a million years ago.

Like a seven-hundred-mile-long, wound-up rubber band, the Cascadia subduction zone holds the potential to unleash a magnitude 9.0 earthquake equal to the one that struck Japan in March 2011—only the sixth of that magnitude worldwide since 1900. The only type of tectonic action known to produce magnitude 9.0 earthquakes is subduction, and the Cascadia zone has flexed its muscle in the geologically recent past. In January 1700, a temblor estimated at 8.7 to 9.2 unleashed a tsunami that reached Japan.

Historically, at least thirteen 8.0-or-higher quakes have struck at intervals of three hundred to nine hundred years. Greater Seattle may still have some breathing room, or may not.

Second gear, still slow but faster than the sporadic shuffling of the tectonic deck, is ice. The Mountain wears a cape of twenty-six glaciers covering thirty-five square miles, more than on any other U.S. peak outside Alaska, each of them inexorably grinding stone to powder. Though moving slowly, they work 24/7/365; so, like a small amount of money invested fortuitously, their long-term gains are impressive. Over the past six thousand years, moving ice has shaved a thousand feet off the mountaintop.

Like most of Earth's glaciers, almost all of Rainier's are shrinking, a direct and escalating consequence of a warming climate. Researchers have estimated that The Mountain lost 18 percent of its ice volume just from 2003 to 2009. Satellite photos taken in 2002 show Rainier's

Nisqually, Winthrop, Tahoma, South Tahoma, and Carbon glaciers at or approaching their historical minimum size—and those are among the biggest. Some, like the Pyramid and Van Trump, have shriveled to "wasting" glaciers, essentially perennial snowfields.

Receding glaciers leave behind steep-sided, barren ridges of rubble called moraines. Because of the brittle nature of igneous rock, moraines on a volcano crumble under any disturbance, whether a climber's boot or a heavy rainstorm. The clatter of falling rocks is an ever-present soundtrack on Mount Rainier.

Flowing water represents third gear. Mount Rainier gives birth to seven rivers and a vast vascular system of 470 waterways within park boundaries, fed by one of the planet's most prodigious water cycles.

All big mountains create their own weather. In a process known as orographic lift, clouds rise as they hit a peak and cool rapidly, often pushing their relative humidity to 100 percent, the point at which precipitation occurs. Sitting so close to the Pacific's prolific moisture pipeline, Rainier attracts bloated fronts barreling in off the ocean like paper clips to a magnet. Average annual rainfall in the park ranges from seventy-five inches on the east side, in Rainier's rain shadow, to 126 inches on the west side—two to three times as much as in famously gloomy Seattle.

At higher elevations, much of that precipitation falls as snow. Paradise, at 5,400 feet on the peak's south side, averages fifty-eight feet annually. Its single-winter record of 93.5 feet in 1971–72 ranks second in the world. All that precipitation transforms Rainier every spring into a 100-square-mile public water fountain. Like the human body, The Mountain appears solid, but is largely defined by water.

And here's the crux point, the pivotal reality around which all human concerns in this park revolve: everything that falls off The Mountain eventually winds up in its rivers. And there's an awful lot of it.

Which leads us to fourth gear, the natural force responsible for the most abrupt, violent, and deadly landscape overhauls on Mount Rainier: floods, including their close relative, lahars. Deadly tsunamis of mud, boulders, and uprooted trees, lahars are as much solid as liquid and can charge down valleys at up to sixty miles per hour. In recent years, especially, park managers have developed a deep respect for and fear of both of those purveyors of destruction.

Given the copious snowfall, it's no surprise when, even in the first week of August, we come upon tongues of snow extending three hundred feet or more down gentle slopes, left over from last winter and spring.

Nate and Alex shuck off their packs, take running starts, and "ski" down one snowfield. They call out, "Come and ski with us, Dad!" I glance at my watch: 5:00 p.m. We have another ninety minutes of hiking to reach Cataract Camp, tonight's campsite. I sense weariness and hunger lurking nearby like patient vultures, waiting to swoop in on my kids.

But how often do we get to ski in August? I run out onto the snow to join them.

BY MORNING, THE CLOUDS have come to us, inundating the treetops—water floating on air like ice on a pond, entrapping us below the surface. Fog makes the forest loom bigger and more alien. It muffles sound as effectively as a cloud-size pillow. I love a fog-enshrouded forest.

Although the skies are threatening rain, everyone's in great spirits. We leave Cataract Camp by midmorning, following a rocky, sometimes muddy footpath to a rendezvous with the lowest, longest, fattest river of ice in the continental U.S.

Shortly after turning onto the Wonderland Trail, we reach the Carbon River, which we must cross on a bouncy, 200-foot-long suspension bridge with three thin steel cables for side rails. A sign warns, "One person on bridge at a time" and "Do not bounce or shake bridge!" Larry had hiked ahead of us and waits on the other side. Nate eagerly strides over it first. Penny protests, "I hate suspension bridges," then shuffles slowly across after Nate. Alex and I will walk it together, a strategy perhaps equally reassuring to both of us.

Alex stares at the bridge in silence. Then she turns to me and says, in an apparent attempt to comfort one of us, "I don't think you'll fall into that river."

"You don't think so?" I ask her. "Why not?"

She points toward the raging white water. "Well, you see that waterfall there? Can you imagine yourself going over it?"

"I'd rather not imagine that," I admit.

"Well, if you can't imagine it, then it probably won't happen!" she says, raising both palms upturned in the universal sign for "Duh!"

Her elusive logic satisfies her. So I thank her for putting me at ease, and we inch across the wobbly structure. She does not stumble or hesitate—though partway across, when I ask how she's feeling, she admits, "dizzy." Through the inch-wide gaps between the bridge's six-inch-wide slats, I look down at the white water twelve feet below our heels.

The swirling, gray waters resemble very liquid cement much more than they do a mountain stream. That muddiness comes from "glacial flour," the fine silt from ground-up stone that glaciers release into their outlet rivers. The tons of silt carried downstream even give the river a different sound, a cross between the roar of white water and a load of sand pouring out of a dump truck. Like every waterway originating in a glacier on this volcano, the Carbon hauls truckloads of The Mountain downstream every hour of every day, year after year.

LESS THAN A HALF mile beyond the bridge, we stop for lunch on trailside rocks overlooking the snout of the Carbon Glacier, which terminates in a cracked, nearly vertical wall of dirty, blue-gray ice at least a hundred feet tall. That snout sits at 3,500 feet above sea level, lower than any other glacial ice in the Lower 48—a testament to the enormous volume of snow feeding the upper glacier. There, snowflakes compressed by new snow accumulating atop them transform into ice crystals within a few years. Then they ride a conveyor belt that extends for 5.7 miles and achieves a maximum thickness of seven hundred feet—both numbers also unmatched in the contiguous U.S. Encased in it are frozen molecules that floated earthward around the time Columbus sailed for the New World. The journey from upper glacier to snout takes several hundred years for a crystal in Rainier's north-side glaciers. Conversely, The Mountain's southerly glaciers move much faster because of their warmer exposure; an identical crystal will exit the Nisqually within about thirty years.

At the Carbon Glacier's toe, a horizontal crack constantly vomits the murky, roiling river into a bed that bears little resemblance to most rivers that do not originate in a glacier. A jumble of rocks virtually devoid of growth, the riverbed spans an area at least ten times the width of the flowing water, indicating just how much the Carbon can swell when it floods, as it has in the recent past.

Given time, most rivers slice ineluctably deeper into the land. But in rivers birthed from moving ice, riverbeds aggrade, or rise, with all the debris filling them. Occasionally, aggradation occurs suddenly in the form of a lahar, also known as a debris flow. It's not uncommon for one debris flow to jack up a riverbed's elevation by inches or even feet.

About 5,600 years ago, Rainier's summit and northeast face collapsed in a massive landslide accompanied by volcanic eruptions, an event known as the Osceola Mudflow. It decapitated The Mountain, knocking its height from somewhere around 16,000 feet—which would make it the highest summit in the Lower 48 today, by a substantial margin—down to a bit lower than its current height of 14,411 feet. (It has since regained some three hundred feet through sporadic volcanic eruptions, the last of which occurred in the 1800s.) A colossal muddy wave roared down the White River Valley, depositing debris six hundred feet deep over an area of 130 square miles and reaching Puget Sound. If a lahar that big struck tomorrow, it would wipe out the communities of Kent, Auburn, Orting, Enumclaw, and Renton, and possibly parts of Seattle, and send tsunamis across Puget Sound.

Most lahars are much smaller, but nonetheless very dangerous. Lahars triggered by the 1980 eruption of Mount St. Helens tore down bridges on the Toutle River, killing motorists, and blocked the shipping channel of the Columbia River seventy miles downstream.

In recent years, scientists have discovered that Rainier's riverbeds are aggrading at a staggering rate of six to twelve inches per decade. On The Mountain's south side, the Nisqually River's bed has risen thirty-eight feet since 1910. The historic community of Longmire, home to park offices and visitor services, now sits twenty-nine feet lower than the Nisqually River bottom, protected from obliteration by a manmade levee, like an alpine New Orleans. Depending on the Nisqually's level at any time, its waters usually charge past Longmire more than thirty feet above the streets.

Still, only one type of flood has ever overtopped the Longmire levee: a glacial-outburst flood. Also known by its Icelandic term, *jökulhlaup*, it is caused by water backing up and forming a lake inside a stagnant glacier, the pressure of which eventually triggers an explosive release. The last one at Rainier was in the 1950s. There are photos from that disaster of river water flowing down the streets of Longmire. Paul Kennard, Mount Rainier National Park's geomorphologist, or river specialist, told me the lower Nisqually Glacier shows signs of stagnating, moving only a few inches a year rather than a normal several inches per day. Park officials fear a lake may be growing inside the ice, setting the stage for a catastrophic jökulhlaup.

One tributary of the Nisqually, Van Trump Creek, didn't see a debris flow in the park's first 101 years; from 2001 through 2006, four careened down it, one of which raised the Nisqually riverbed by five and a half feet. In the park's northeast corner, the White River's bed has aggraded four feet just since 2003. It now sits sixteen feet higher than White River Road. Acres of old-growth Douglas fir, cedar, and hemlock trees are suffocating beneath silt deposited by the White. If it breaches its levee, at least two miles of road will become river.

The era of climate change has made the term "100-year flood" a dark joke among managers at Mount Rainier National Park and on other Pacific Northwest public lands.

Warmer temperatures put storms on steroids. Experts, including the Union of Concerned Scientists, expect that higher average temperatures will crank up the hydrological cycle, because air holds more moisture as it warms. One 2005 study forecast a 140 percent leap in "extreme precipitation events" in the Pacific Northwest, primarily between November and January, when rainstorms can abruptly liquefy wasting glaciers and new, unconsolidated snow, exacerbating flooding. Some of those autumn and early-winter storms come in unusually warm—they're called Pineapple Express storms—melting snow more rapidly. When I asked Portland State University researcher Andrew Fountain about that type of storm, he said, gravely, "You're going to see more of that."

Winter has changed, with more rain instead of snow. Oregon State University climatologist Anne Nolin predicted in a 2006 paper that, by midcentury, 22 percent of Oregon's Cascades and 60 percent of Washington's Olympic Mountains—an area exceeding 3,500 square miles—could see rain falling at elevations that now get snow in winter. Even where the white stuff holds out, it will fall in temperatures nearer to freezing, making it more susceptible to rapid melting.

Kennard told me his job entails dealing with "flood damage that has occurred or is about to occur." In a scientist's tone of detached objectivity, he described for me the guillotine blade suspended over the park. There has been a growing number of debris flows—about four a year as of the middle of last decade. Conditions are ripe for a cataclysmic flood. But what he feared most was what nobody yet knows: how severe the biggest storms will get in a warmer climate.

Floods and lahars, fourth speed in the engine that perpetually shapes and reshapes Mount Rainier, are becoming turbocharged.

FROM THE CARBON RIVER Bridge to Mystic Lake, tonight's destination, we face a four-and-a-half-mile, three-thousand-foot climb. I look up at the cloud ceiling; it's nowhere near three thousand feet above us. We'll hike uphill into the fog and rain long before reaching camp—with the temperature in the fifties. I'm hoping it won't be too miserable for my kids.

As we hike, I watch Nate and Alex negotiate this rugged terrain. Walking a trail of slippery rocks, traversing a narrow log bridge over a white-water creek, or rock-hopping a stream, they move nimbly, without apprehension or a break in the conversation. This is as familiar to them now as the sidewalk on the way to school.

During a break, we discover a banana slug as long as one of Nate's or Alex's hands. A little while later, we pass a fresh pile of black bear poop in the middle of the trail. "Maybe we'll bump into a big brrrroooo-in out here!" I say in mock fright. Nate and Alex roll their eyes.

By midafternoon, the rain begins. We put on breathable waterproof jackets with hoods up, pull waterproof covers over our packs, and keep walking. Penny and Alex get ahead while Nate and I talk and shoot some photos. I hand him the compact umbrella I brought, seeing its immediate psychological benefit as his eyes widen when I pull it out. I think he's as enamored of the quick-release button that snaps it open as of the protection it offers.

At one point, Nate observes, "My feet are pulsing." But his tone is more fascination than complaint.

The steady, windless rain continues throughout our two-hour walk to Mystic Lake—on the same stretch of the Wonderland Trail that I hiked during that violent storm in October 2003, the same section of trail destroyed in November 2006, since repaired in a project that took months. But the Carbon River still flows down two miles of its eponymous road, which may never reopen.

At our camp in early evening, we hurriedly pitch tents, dive inside, and wait. Light rain in the backcountry can inspire a powerful optimism: This will pass, I tell myself. It doesn't. Finally, Penny and I venture outside and cook dinner beneath conifer boughs that grant a little protection from the shower. Larry joins us, and the kids come out when dinner's ready.

Larry has been climbing Northwest mountains for thirty years. After the nine months of raw, gray drizzle that Pacific Northwest residents endure from fall through early summer, he and generations of his regional neighbors looked forward to dry, sunny, glorious weather from July to September, with none of the humidity or severe heat afflicting other parts of the country.

Gesturing toward our gloomy August sky, Larry tells us that that old climate regime seems a thing of the past. "For several summers, it's been much more erratic," he says. "Rain during summer. Erratic in winters, too."

It's also been hotter. In a region where highs in the seventies were long the norm and many buildings lack air conditioning, a summer 2009 heat wave baked Seattle and Portland in temps of over a hundred degrees Fahrenheit. The July 29, 2009, high of 103 degrees Fahrenheit in Seattle was the hottest temperature in the city since record-keeping began in 1894. That mark may not stand for long: average temperatures in the Pacific Northwest are predicted to increase a half degree Fahrenheit per decade through midcentury—three times the region's rate of warming during the twentieth century.

Later, we retreat to the tents, soon dropping off to the lulling sound of rain softly drumming on our nylon roofs. I fall through a trap door into the dream-flooded, deep unconsciousness of a sleeping child, and wake up feeling as if I'd slept for weeks.

THE FIRST RAINDROPS OF the most destructive storm in Mount Rainier National Park's 109-year history fell on Sunday afternoon, November 5, 2006. Pacific Northwest winter storms typically blow in on polar jet streams and flush through quickly. But a shift in the jet stream carried this one up from the subtropics; it may have originated as a typhoon in the Sea of Japan. Pregnant with moisture, it stalled over the region. Rain fell as in a monsoon, nearly eighteen inches in thirty-six hours—the equivalent of fifteen feet of snow. Unseasonably warm, this Pineapple Express dumped rain even at Camp Muir, at ten thousand feet. Snow that had recently fallen above eight thousand feet melted abruptly, swelling rivers even more.

The extent of flood devastation stunned even people who had worked in the park for decades. Major sections of road were gone, including four washouts on WA 123, one deep enough to drop a seven-story building into it. Six debris flows scored Rainier's slopes. The Nisqually River devoured most of Longmire's levee—coming within inches of buildings—and swept five acres of Sunshine Point Campground out of existence. Winds as strong as a Category 3 hurricane tore the roofs off two fire lookouts.

The Wonderland Trail took hits in more than thirty locations, including damage to the Tahoma Creek suspension bridge, which rises a hundred feet above the creek. In 2007, parts of the trail were closed throughout the hiking season. For the first time since the trail's completion in 1915, backpackers could not hike the entire route.

Dubbing it the Great Flood of November 2006, officials characterized it as a 400-year flood; the last comparable event in the geologic record occurred that long ago. Never before had a storm affected every road, every trail in the park. Repairs would cost $24 million. The park was closed to private vehicles for a record six months; even world wars and the ash fallout from the 1980 eruption of Mount St. Helens had closed it for only a few days.

The following summer, I saw mind-boggling devastation while backpacking here: trails kneecapped by landslides, numerous washouts, and thousands of 100-foot-tall trees heaped like matchsticks. We visited the former site of Pyramid Creek Camp, along the Wonderland Trail, which had been buried beneath a tangle of mud-caked trees two feet in diameter by a lahar. Fortunately, no one was there when it hit, for it was clear no one could have survived.

Moraines left behind by retreating glaciers eventually stabilize with new vegetation, creating fewer debris flows. But with glacial recession a certainty for decades to come, Mount Rainier and other Cascade volcanoes will continue acting as incubators for lahars.

And the next monster storm may not be far off. In fact, another did strike the Pacific Northwest just a year after Rainier's record floods. On December 3, 2007, on Washington's Olympic Peninsula, fourteen inches of rain fell in forty-eight hours. Flooding and mudslides mangled roads and campgrounds, high winds flattened thousands of trees, and rivers reached 500-year-flood levels. Combined damages at Olympic National Park and National Forest topped $19 million.

Make that four hundred-year-or-greater floods in the Pacific Northwest within twelve years.

WE AWAKEN ON OUR final morning to a surprise: no sound of rain on the tent, not even the occasional splat of water dripping from trees. By the time we hit the trail, sunlight slashes through a disintegrating overcast, illuminating steam clouds rising from a forest reeking of humus and opportunistic fungi.

Birds sing. The dense forest sifts the raucous clamor of the West Fork White River to a smooth, pleasing white noise. Penny and Alex play a word game. Nate skips and bounds ahead of us, dashing through his fertile imagination. Nine miles and a two-thousand-foot climb separate us from our car. But the sky smiles benevolently on us today, and we're smiling back.

We carefully cross a log footbridge over a foaming, gray, roaring Winthrop Creek. Puffy clouds march past the massive Winthrop Glacier. Then we're ascending through more forest, mossy and littered with rotting deadfall. At a rocky outcropping overlooking the Winthrop's hundred-foot-high flanks, we stop and try to visually digest the Walmart of ice within our field of view—and contemplate that it represents merely a tiny piece of the whole, something like seeing a few ribs in a body three and a half miles long and comprising 18.5 billion cubic feet.

After a lunch break, Larry, Penny, and Nate start hiking, while Alex and I get delayed by several minutes as I reload food into my pack, tie her boots, wait for her to pee, and heft my ungainly load onto my back. Twenty steps later, we confront an enormous tree that has fallen across the trail.

Alex crawls easily underneath it. I try to clamber over the top, something I've probably done five hundred times. But I'm not thinking about my additional, top-heavy weight. A foot slips on the slick log. My pack throws me as if I've been blindsided by a linebacker, and I'm airborne. I tumble and crash hard to earth, my legs in the air like an upended turtle.

I curse under my breath—then remember that my seven-year-old daughter, whose reaction I can't see right now, just watched her father take a nasty fall. "I'm okay!" I call out too enthusiastically, like my fall was an experiment and I was generally pleased with the results. Panting and struggling, I roll over and push myself up onto my feet, brush off the mud and moss, and look at Alex.

"Ready?" she asks. We exchange smiles and she holds my hand as we start walking.

A little while later, icing a few swollen, throbbing knuckles on my left hand in frigid Granite Creek, I notice a big dent in the stainless-steel water bottle in an outside pocket on my pack. I apparently landed on it. Larry says, "That could have been your kidneys." I nod, thinking about the implications for my family should I get hurt out here.

By midafternoon, we reach a pass at the apex of our two-thousand-foot climb. Before us spreads the sort of breathtaking scene that inspired the designation, in 1899, of Mount Rainier as America's fifth national park. The Wonderland Trail meanders across a vast field sprayed with the colors of lupine, phlox, and pink mountain heather. Breaths of cool fog bob above Berkeley Park, a vibrantly green cirque below us. Small copses of conifer trees grow not much taller than a human, many of them "flagged," meaning their branches all point in the same direction, with the prevailing winds.

As we walk the last few miles of wide-open, gently rolling terrain, the clouds part to reveal The Mountain. I gaze up at Rainier's tattered and torn cape of glaciers, too immense for our eyes to accurately interpret its scale; and it seems at once impossible, amazing, and frightening that we are capable of affecting the climate in a way that alters the topography of this mountain.

What seems most certain for Mount Rainier National Park's future is greater uncertainty: bigger storms; roads, trails, and bridges washed out randomly; campsites occasionally erased from the landscape. While park managers and workers do a magnificent job of maintaining the infrastructure in an extremely volatile environment, the surrender of the Carbon River Road to the Carbon River shows that we cannot spend enough money or wield enough technology to win every battle against nature—not when nature grows increasingly unpredictable and violent. Future storms will alter this park in ways we cannot anticipate.

Plus, at Rainier and other Northwest volcanoes, the drain plug has already been pulled on processes—glacial recession, aggradation, debris flows—that cannot be restrained.

As Paul Kennard told me, "Because of the glaciers receding, our problems keeping the roads open will be greater." And Kevin Bacher, who manages the park's volunteers, pointed out that, as riverbeds rise, "it takes less of a flood to come to our facilities. These are issues that could eventually make the 2006 flood look small. It's very sobering here in Longmire, where I sit in my office next to a river that, if it breaches that dike, might be flowing past my second-floor window."

What's happening here spins a narrative different from the typical global-warming story, in which changes often come too slowly to perceive. Floods and debris flows are violent, catastrophic—and poignantly symbolic. What could be a more powerful metaphor for climatic anarchy than a lahar coursing downhill, carrying inestimable tons of rock and trees, wielding the strength to erase roads and small towns and change the course of rivers?

As much as anything, Rainier's story illustrates how the impacts of climate change aren't always gradual. Sometimes they're sudden and very, very messy.

Sometimes, overnight, they can leave a place in ruins.

Nate and Alex peek through driftwood on the beach in Olympic National Park, Washington.

CHAPTER 5

ALONG A WILD COAST

AUGUST 2010

The waves are crashing closer to us.

This anxious thought comes to me uninvited as we scramble, slip, and stumble over a beach tiled with abrasive conglomerate boulders, all coated green with wet, slick kelp and barnacles. Every step feels tenuous, made more unsteady by our heavy backpacks.

Another set of waves smashes the rocks on my left, seawater slithering up between them to within a couple of feet of the boulder I'm balanced atop. The waters recede to feed the next wave set, which inches a little closer. Thirty feet to my right, the beach butts up against a crumbling cliff that stretches ahead of us for a half mile. A flat, gray cloud ceiling hovers just overhead, kissing the forest canopy atop the cliff. It seems to make our shrinking space between ocean and earthen wall feel a little more claustrophobic.

Beside me, Alex slips off a rock, lands hard on her behind. She meets my look of concern, chirps, "I'm all right," pushes herself to her feet, and accepts my hand. We continue on, step by agonizingly slow, measured step.

Perhaps fifty feet ahead, Penny and Nate stagger along, arms outstretched for balance. And not much beyond them, Penny's brother, Tom Beach, standing more than six feet and lean, and Tom's fifteen-year-old son, Daniel, with hair to his collarbone and a six-foot frame bursting with teenage growth, move with similar caution.

I glance at my watch: almost noon. According to the tide table for Washington's Olympic coast, a copy of which is in my pocket, we still have an hour before high tide inundates this rocky shore up to the cliffs, carrying off any misguided terrestrial creatures still on the beach. On a rational level, I know we have plenty of time to get beyond this minefield of greasy rocks to the safety of the wide, sandy beach ahead. But when waves crash at my feet, closing the gap to a cliff as I plod forward hand in hand with my child, rational thought is as easy to hold onto as water in one palm.

On the list of specific threats to the lives and limbs of my children that I had compiled before we began this series of park adventures, somehow, getting swept out to sea by an incoming tide had never popped up on my radar.

This strikes me now as a conspicuous oversight.

We are ninety minutes into a three-day backpacking trip along part of the longest wilderness coastline remaining in the contiguous United States. On the outer edge of the Olympic Peninsula—that thick forearm that the state of Washington raises defiantly toward the battering Pacific—Olympic National Park protects seventy-three miles of undeveloped seashore. There are no hotel strips, warehouse-size homes, fried-seafood joints, or moped rentals. The rocky beaches and sea cliffs look essentially no different to us than they did to the first people who settled here at least six thousand years ago, living off shellfish, salmon, and marine mammals hunted from cedar canoes.

On this windward side of the Olympic Mountains, twelve to fourteen feet of rain a year sustain one of Earth's largest virgin temperate rainforests, an ecosystem possibly containing more living biomass than anywhere else in the world. Sitka spruce and western red cedar soar to 150 feet tall, with diameters of ten to fifteen feet, while Douglas fir and western hemlock climb to well over two hundred feet. Ferns grow so densely that you rarely glimpse the ground. Mosses carpet every rock and trunk and hang from every limb. Thirty miles inland, the Olympic Mountains reach their apex in 7,980-foot Mount Olympus, which, thanks to abundant snowfall, supports the third-largest system of glaciers in the Lower 48, despite standing little more than half the height of Mount Rainier.

Salmon spawn in wild rivers. Bald eagles, tufted puffins, and seabirds thrive. Offshore upwellings of nutrient-rich cold water in summer nurture a food chain ranging from the foundation species of all life—phytoplankton and zooplankton—to invertebrates; fish of all sizes; seals; sea lions; sea otters; and humpback, gray, minke, and blue whales. Over five hundred known species of marine invertebrates and seaweeds live here, more than anywhere else on North America's west coast, from Alaska to Panama. This diversity drove the preservation of 3,300 square miles of Pacific Ocean as the Olympic Coast National Marine Sanctuary.

All along this wild coast, land and sea engage in an ancient contest in which the land has no hope to win, only to forestall its inevitable demise. In this epic battle, the malevolent sea pummels the shore relentlessly. Waves roll stones up and down beaches like billions of dice, tear down headlands, and topple giant trees into the surf.

But the land doesn't give up without at least a good metaphorical fight. Sprinkled liberally along this coast, scores of stone pinnacles—called sea stacks—rise out of the ocean. While it's tempting to imagine them as eternal features of the seascape, they were once part of the mainland. Composed of harder sandstone than much of the headlands that face the Pacific, the sea stacks remained standing after softer rock and dirt surrounding them eroded away. Some lie close enough to the beach to walk to them at low tide; others erupt from the sea hundreds of yards offshore. Some are no taller than a small house and composed of bare rock, others are two hundred feet or taller and topped by a thin skin of soil and grass and a copse of trees, or a solitary tree.

Remnants of the former shoreline, they stand as stark, lonely symbols of how the past cannot be retrieved, only reflected on from a distance.

Another wave set crashes into the rocks, nearly licking our boots. I steer Alex higher up the beach, where the rocks are bigger and more difficult—and slower—to maneuver over and around.

And it occurs to me, as the tide creeps in on us, that we are walking through a window on the future of the wildest American coast south of Alaska.

HAPPILY, WE GET BEYOND the rocky shore without the tide sweeping anyone out to sea. Crossing nearly a mile of damp, sandy beach, we stop below another wall of earth.

A thick strand of hemp rope dangles more than a hundred feet down this steep, eroding embankment. A ladder of wooden steps built into the muddy ground rises in tandem with the rope. This rope ladder marks the start of a three-mile-long overland trail through the rainforest. It will lead us over Hoh Head, an impassable section of the southern Olympic coast where cliffs rise straight out of the pounding ocean. It's the longest of four such trails we will take around headlands on this three-day, eighteen-mile hike from the Hoh River north to La Push Road.

"Oh, there's a slug! There's ANOTHER slug!"

Nate spews this animated play-by-play as I follow Alex and him up the rope ladder, bracing myself to—in theory—catch a tumbling kid. To my relief and no doubt that of Penny, who watches with great interest from below, they do not test my fielding skills, scaling it easily. With Daniel and Tom leading, we then slip and slide along a footpath of ankle-deep muck to another rope ladder going straight up an even steeper wall of earth sprouting junglelike vegetation. For about a quarter mile, we ascend at this extreme angle before the path finally levels off somewhat.

Still, throughout its length, this overland trail undulates frequently through dips of twenty and thirty feet that are as tiring to navigate as climbing and descending a couple flights of stairs every ten minutes. Mud smothers the trail, as unavoidable as the rain that made it. Impolite and unselfconscious, the muck makes sucking and belching noises under our boots and hurls globs that smear our legs, arms, and clothes. We sink into knee-deep brown holes. I watch the kids walk toe-to-heel along slick logs spanning bogs into which I can imagine them disappearing.

The spruce and cedar tower overhead, stretching roots as thick as anacondas over the ground. Some grow atop the mind-boggling numbers of fat, dead trunks that are called "nurse logs" because they essentially function as soil for so much new growth. Those elevated young trees send roots straight down to the soil; over decades, the dead trunks below rot away, leaving a mature tree standing on vertical roots as if atop several stilts.

Ducking under tilting trees and pushing through vegetation overgrowing the trail, Nate informs me, "This is like bushwhacking. I need a machete." I form an image of my son lopping off a foot out here, and make a mental note: offer him no concession on the machete thing.

For the last mile or so of today's hike, Alex shares with me a nonstop monologue that ranges nimbly from what she wants for Christmas—Polly Pockets, American Girl dolls, Legos, the list goes on—to which friend she plans to invite for a sleepover once we are home, and the script of a play she's writing in which she will star as a princess and I will play a wizard king. "Don't you think being a wizard king would be better than being a backpacking writer?" she asks me. I can't argue against that.

Midafternoon, having taken five hours to walk five miles, we drop our packs at a campsite in the forest near Mosquito Creek. Our camp terminates abruptly at a ragged edge of eroded bluff dropping precipitously more than a hundred feet to the rocky beach. Waves crash loudly, each one dragging so many stones over the beach that it sounds like a rockslide on a mountain. Two sea stacks ignore the nuisance tide nipping at their heels. Nate and Alex take off immediately toward the creek and beach.

After setting up camp, I leave Penny, Tom, and Daniel reading or napping in their tents and walk five minutes down the trail to where it tumbles onto the beach. Here, as all along this coast, enormous tree trunks litter the ground in heaps at the high-tide line. Stripped of their bark and most branches and bleached white by the ocean, they could be bones—if there had ever lived a creature with a hundred-foot-long femur.

Under the low, gray ceiling, Alex and Nate wade knee-deep in their sandals in a tiny lagoon where Mosquito Creek backs up behind the beach. Already, they have constructed sand castles and an armada of a half dozen driftwood battleships and carriers. Seeing me, they launch into exhaustive explanations of their ships' features: mud-and-stick anti-aircraft guns, river-stone amphibious vehicles, and twig fighter jets. Tonight, after they have spent three hours in this water, I'll touch their hands and feet, a little test I do to check whether they're slightly hypothermic, and their skin will feel like meat pulled from a refrigerator.

I look out at the invading tide, which at its high point barely spills into this brackish lagoon. Then I turn around and look at Mosquito Creek's mouth, emerging from a steep-sided ravine; and I see the Pacific Ocean someday crawling far up this creek, chewing easily into these soft embankments, swallowing this tidal pond.

THE LAND AND SEA engage in a second kind of contest on the Olympic coast, one in which the land fares somewhat better than it does against the inexorable onslaught of waves that isolates the sea stacks.

Operating on a few levels, this game explains a couple of curious truths about the peninsula: First, why one can find ocean fossils at seven thousand feet in the Olympic Mountains. And why, even as worldwide sea level rises—about seven inches in the past century, currently creeping upward by about one-tenth of an inch per year and accelerating—the peninsula uplifts at basically the same speed. The explanation lies in physical processes that reach deep into the Earth's crust and history.

Thirteen thousand years ago, the Olympic Peninsula lay beneath the terminus of the thousand-foot-thick Cordilleran Ice Sheet. Since the ice began retreating, the land has risen at the unhurried pace of geology, still rebounding today.

Another, much older movement of rock helps shape the peninsula's story. About 35 million years ago, two plates of the planet's crust collided here, with the Juan de Fuca oceanic plate sliding beneath the North American continental plate. Called subduction, this process forces the oceanic plate deep into the Earth, birthing Cascade Range volcanoes and the tectonic instability that triggers the most destructive earthquakes and tsunamis.

On top of glacial isostatic rebound and plate tectonics, the peninsula's geology owes much of its composition to dead shellfish. For eons, an awful lot of sea creatures dying and sinking to the ocean floor have piled up in sedimentary layers atop the oceanic plate. As the oceanic plate dives beneath the continental plate, those layers get scraped off like peanut butter off a dish, Steven Fradkin told me. Olympic National Park's coastal ecologist, Fradkin then delivered the punch line: "The Olympic Mountains are basically a lot of peanut butter."

While the waters of nearby Puget Sound may come up another foot or more in this century, the Olympic coast will likely experience a net sea-level rise of about two inches, according to a 2008 report from the University of Washington Climate Impacts Group (UW CIG) and the Washington Department of Ecology.

But the coast nonetheless faces many of the impacts of rising seas because of another fact: it cannot duck its age-old nemesis, the waves, and they are getting larger.

"One of the major predictions of climate change is we are going to see bigger storms more frequently," Fradkin noted.

If daily tide fluctuations and small storms whittle away at the coastline, tempests take a hatchet to it. And the Pacific Ocean brews many a tempest that makes first landfall in the Pacific Northwest, at the Olympic coast. Weather systems from the Bering Sea to Polynesia send ocean swells propagating thousands of miles across the Pacific, without interruption. As if to return the favor, peripatetic waves blend waters of radically different temperatures, creating the huge pressure differentials that foment storms.

Explorers and sailors of the wooden-ship era knew the terror of a major ocean storm off the Olympic coast—at least 150 shipwrecks sit on the ocean bottom here. Pieces of wrecks more than a century old wash up onto Olympic beaches every year. Storm winds whip up the water's surface, magnifying waves and actually lifting the sea higher. Like artillery laying siege to a fortress, waves pound the shoreline inexhaustibly, clawing at eroding bluffs until earth and trees landslide into the sea.

A warmer climate creates greater temperature ranges across the ocean, and thus larger pressure differentials, spawning more powerful gales that are pumped up further because warmer air holds more moisture. The Pacific Northwest's coast receives an added amplifier in winter in the form of a prevailing northward wind that pushes ocean water toward shore. Abetted by the Earth's rotation, these winds raise Washington's mean wintertime sea level twenty inches higher than the summer level—and more than thirty inches higher during an El Niño, the quasi-cyclical warming of the tropical Pacific. Researchers are trying to figure out whether a 60 percent jump in the variability of El Niño events in the past fifty years is tied to global warming. Some scientists worry that, if El Niño deviates beyond some unknown tipping point and settles into a new equilibrium, dramatic climate shifts will escalate.

A 2004 U.S. Geological Survey report rated half of the park coastline at high or very high vulnerability to sea-level rise—the erosion that Fradkin described to me. The UW CIG predicts that impacts of climate change—like increased winter rainfall, warmer winters, and higher seas—will magnify landslides, coastal erosion, and river flooding.

While much of the southern stretch we're hiking is well armored by rocky headlands, the Mosquito Creek area is a "soft coastline," Fradkin said. "I would expect to see a lot more mass wasting of the uplands there and wave action causing slope failure."

Sandy areas on the southern coast, like Ruby Beach and Kalaloch, and most of the northern Olympic coast, including popular Shi Shi Beach, are all rated highly vulnerable.

Waves hammer shores all over the world, and the Olympic coast has always been a dynamic environment. Some of its beaches routinely transform from sandy in summer to rocky in winter and back again.

But bigger waves hitting more frequently will tear it down faster. As Fradkin told me, "Waves have a major potential to change the shoreline, eroding it and redistributing what's there."

EARLY ON OUR SECOND morning, Tom and I stand almost motionless at the torn edge of our campsite where the land falls away over the eroding bluff. I cradle a mug of hot tea in my hands, and he a coffee. We stare out at the fog-shrouded sea, though not with the longing of wool-clad, early mariners to explore the vast, daunting unknown. Ours is more the longing of down jacket–clad, twenty-first-century backpackers who wouldn't mind a little sunshine.

"There's an island out there," Tom says. Alexander Island, a finger of forest-covered rock a mile offshore, has materialized from the impenetrable fog. A moment later, it disappears again. We shift our gazes to a rocky headland protruding from the bluff maybe a quarter mile down the beach, a spit of stone thinning visibly on its inland side—a sea stack in utero.

"Looks like the weather hasn't changed."

Penny mutters this unenthusiastically as she emerges from the tent she and Alex are sharing. She is almost literally correct. The temperature probably has not shifted more than a few degrees since yesterday, and the fog seems as durable as Twinkies. Penny digs out her coffee press. I don't pursue further conversation yet, having learned to give her a wide berth until she's had at least one mug.

Alex springs from the tent minutes after Penny. My daughter awakens every morning as if met by the surprising sight of every doll in the American Girl collection magically appearing in her bed. She excitedly spouts plot details from the book she's reading. Among my pack's substantial contents are three chapter books for Alex; she will finish them before this three-day hike is over.

Another forty minutes elapse before Nate crawls from our tent. He shuffles toward us emitting low growls of general displeasure, like a bear shaking off a hibernation in which he just could not get comfortable. As a first order of business, Nate pronounces, apropos of nothing, that he will hike not one step today until granted an unspecified satisfactory amount of time to prepare the kids' Mosquito Creek fleet for imminent war.

My son, I am certain, is destined for a coffee dependency. I promise him and Alex some creek time, and then silently contemplate whether caffeine could really be all that unhealthy for a nine-year-old.

Daniel, an inveterate teenage sleeper, remains unconscious until Tom prods him with the news that we're packing up. Then our long-haired young companion staggers from their tent with the single most awesome case of bed head that I have ever seen.

Two hours later, with all of our camping gear and food once again stuffed into our backpacks, the six of us stroll across Mosquito Creek where it fans out an inch or two deep over the sand, following the beach north past more deadwood. I wonder which of these tree skeletons were thrown onto the beach by "sneaker waves," anomalous large waves that, every year along the West Coast, catch a few beachgoers off-guard and drag them out to sea. Walking firm sand at low tide, under this overcast, in temperatures that have not budged from the fifties Fahrenheit, we're not even breaking a sweat.

A mile beyond Mosquito Creek, we come upon one of the true delights of a wild coastline.

A boulder about twenty feet tall and wide and twice as long sits in the intertidal zone, the strip of beach that's exposed now, at low tide, and underwater at high tide. Approaching it, we can see that below the high-tide line around the boulder's waist, it is wallpapered with barnacles, sea anemones, starfish colored boldly orange or purple, and thousands of mussels packed shell to shell over the stone's surface. In a shallow moat of seawater partly encircling the rock, anemones open up, each waving dozens of short, green tentacles. Alex and Nate reach out and touch fingertips to the starfish and mussels, my kids actually silenced by fascination.

Forty years from now, Nate and Alex could probably walk up to this same boulder, wading into that emotional riptide where the joy of fond memories mixes with the melancholy of the unrecoverable past. But would they delight in discovering this rock covered with mussels, or feel the profound disappointment of finding it bare?

This rich intertidal zone, with its hundreds of species, exists in a dynamic and fragile ecological niche. Organisms live hours of every day underwater, in temperatures that vary little, between roughly 53 and 59 degrees Fahrenheit; and hours of each day above water. Today, the air deviates negligibly from the water. But in recent summers, daytime highs have spiked to an unusual 95 degrees Fahrenheit—a forty-degree shift occurring within the short time it takes the tide to expose a rocky shore or a boulder.

Records dating to 1948 show that average temperatures at 4,700 feet in the Olympic Mountains have leaped 2.2 degrees Fahrenheit in just sixty years. Fradkin, the coastal ecologist, said that many of these organisms "are not particularly good at dealing with significant changes in temperature." Scientists have reported increasing episodes of seaweed "bleaching," which occurs when seaweed exposed for hours to hot temperatures turns white and dies.

Researchers have also found an increase in ocean acidity off the Olympic coast consistent with the ocean's worldwide average drop in pH of 0.1. "That really affects all these organisms that use calcium to make shells, and most organisms in the ocean use calcium," Fradkin said. As in other coastal environments, like Glacier Bay and the Everglades, rising acidity appears to compromise the ability of creatures that form the base of a complex food chain to build shells, survive, and reproduce.

Walking up the beach again, Nate and I trail behind the others. He starts talking about climate change and speculates that people will become more aware and concerned as cities like New York and Miami face increasingly higher seas. As proud amazement infuses me over having this conversation with my nine-year-old, he says, "I'm really glad you took me here."

I resist the temptation to jokingly ask him, "Who are you and what have you done with my son?" Instead, I wait quietly, sensing that whatever I could say right now might not be as valuable as what he might add. Sure enough, after a pause, Nate says, "Dad, I want you to keep backpacking into your sixties and seventies so that I can take you on trips and bring my kids with us, too." I tell him I hope to do exactly that.

Just as I'm expecting him to deliver the coup de grace that reduces me to a blubbering mess, he spares me. In a seamless return to character, Nate resolutely predicts: "I'm going to invent a teleportation device to replace all the transportation systems that put so much carbon in the atmosphere."

I wonder how many of the scientists I've been interviewing for this book had similar childhood dreams.

LATER THAT SECOND AFTERNOON, I clutch a rope tightly in one hand and lean out over a ladder that hangs down a nearly vertical cliff. Perhaps eighty feet below me, I see what I've expected: several rungs missing from the ladder's bottom.

I had been warned about this rope ladder by both a park ranger and a guidebook author I know. When I asked the writer over coffee whether he thought I could get the kids down safely, he hesitated. "It's fifteen or twenty feet without rungs, vertical. You have to Batman down the rope," he said.

The ranger was slightly more sanguine about our chances of a safe descent: "Well, maybe. Sure, you'll probably be fine, I guess."

I downclimb the ladder to inspect it and leave my pack at the bottom. Where the rungs are missing, the cliff's crumbling face offers terrible footing. But the cliff's angle also tilts slightly less than vertical there; I can easily lower myself with my feet on the cliff, and, I figure, do the same separately with each of my kids just above me to prevent a fall.

Daniel and Tom descend with slow caution but no problem. I go up and down a couple more times separately with Nate, who initially objects to my escort, and Alex, who is content to have me guide her.

"Hey, look who I found!" Penny, the last to come down, yells from the cliff top. Then she tosses down Alex's almost-abandoned stuffed panda, Spotty, and I catch it. Seeing one of their animals plunge eighty feet into my hands, the kids burst into the kind of childish laughter that's so out of proportion but genuine that it goes viral through Tom, Daniel, and me.

Later, at Toleak Point, we pitch tents on the beach for our last night out here. Dozens of offshore stacks conjure the ruins of a flooded city. The fog has lifted slightly, daylight penetrating it as if through a dirty cellar window. A sea otter emerges from nearby Jackman Creek and flops across the sand to the ocean. A harbor seal cavorts in the water thirty feet offshore. When I walk over to explore the sea stacks off the point, a great blue heron lifts off the grassy summit of one stack and beats the air slowly, like a winged dinosaur.

In the evening, after the muddy daylight completes an almost imperceptibly drawn-out fade to night, we retreat to our tents. While Nate flops and kicks through the action movies of his dreams, I listen to the constancy of the ocean's white noise parsing into layers: an unbroken rhythm like sand pouring into a basin, the irregular thunder of waves, and the occasional thump of a wave trapping a pocket of air.

Homo sapiens may have had ample utilitarian motives for settling along coastlines—food sources, an agreeable climate, easy transport. But I suspect we stayed in part because the tide is the world's first and most perfect lullaby.

"I'VE BEEN HERE SINCE 1986, and there were glaciers in this park that I've hiked by that are now gone," Bill Baccus, the park's physical scientist, told me. "When you can start looking at your old photos and seeing how different it looks, it's stunning."

After several trips over the years in the Olympic Mountains, I understand Baccus's perspective. I've camped beside an alpine lake below a mountain slope wearing a few patches of snow in late summer; just fifteen years earlier, the Ferry Glacier extended down that slope into the lake, and fifteen years before that, glacial ice covered that entire basin— there was no lake. I've climbed Mount Olympus, stepping across yawning crevasses that opened deeper into the guts of the Blue Glacier than my partners and I cared to think about. The terminus of that glacier has lost more than 150 feet of its thickness in just twenty-five years.

Four thousand miles of rivers and streams intricately dissect the Olympic Peninsula across twelve major watersheds, many feeding or originating in some of the six hundred mountain lakes. These waters are home to thirty-one species of native freshwater and anadromous fish— the latter being those that migrate up rivers from the sea to breed in freshwater—including all five native Pacific salmon. Rising water temperatures threaten salmon and fish such as trout everywhere because they need cooler waters to survive. In just one example, scientists know that 90 percent or more of bull trout eggs will incubate successfully in water at 36 to 43 degrees Fahrenheit (2 to 6 degrees Celsius), but just 20 percent survive in water at 50 degrees (10 Celsius). Earlier spring snowmelt and runoff will affect aquatic life in ways still largely unknown.

The Olympic marmot, which has whistled at me in subalpine

meadows in the Olympic Mountains, the only place it lives, has declined in population from an estimated two thousand to a bit over eight hundred in just three decades. Suzanne Griffin, who studied them for several years for her PhD dissertation, blames winters of low snowfall. She told me that coyotes, which are not native to the peninsula, cannot travel easily through deep snow. But in winters of lean snowfall, as from 2002 through 2006, coyotes decimate the marmot population. A 2006 study projected that 60 percent of the Olympic Mountains that now receive snowfall in winter will see rain instead by the time Nate and Alex are my age.

It's stunning to contemplate so much change occurring within the brief time it takes for a child to grow up.

On the Olympic coast, record books of human history face as much risk as nature. Fifteen archeological sites have been catalogued on park beaches, including a former village at Toleak Point, where there had been longhouses and a large shell midden, a sort of dump where ancient people discarded shells after consuming their contents. Researchers find evidence in these sites of how subsistence cultures used fish and sea mammals. The most famous of them, a native Makah longhouse village at Cape Alava, was buried by an earthquake-triggered mudslide in January 1700—the same quake that sent titanic tsunamis to Japan. Some sites slightly inland from the active shoreline may date back five thousand years.

All of these human and natural resources could be destroyed, possibly gradually, possibly in one catastrophic event if a big storm hits on a high tide, as happened to a midden south of La Push a few years ago.

"What potentially could be lost? Scientifically, the value is immense. Culturally—I don't know how to put a value on that," park archeologist Dave Conca told me.

The Atlantic, Gulf, and Pacific shorelines of the contiguous United States comprise about five thousand miles—slightly more than the distance to fly from New York to Rio de Janeiro. We have bought, sold, and built upon most of that coast so thoroughly that it bears little resemblance to the thickly forested shores that Christopher Columbus and Captain George Vancouver sailed past. The Olympic coast shines as one of the few that those explorers would recognize. Though we've created parks to preserve it and a handful of other shores like the Everglades and Acadia, our pumping of carbon dioxide into the atmosphere has catalyzed a rapid rise in sea level that will continue for a very long time, accelerating processes that tear down these last virgin coasts.

WALKING ALONG THE BEACH on our last day, under that seemingly perpetual low overcast, I'm busily shooting photos. Penny walks ahead talking with Tom and Daniel. The kids trail behind me. Nate hops onto and over the scattered big rocks on the beach; a dirty old buoy that he salvaged dangles from his backpack, destined for a new life in the cluttered museum of boyhood that is his bedroom. Alex walks beside him, the two of them talking and laughing, lost in conversation.

Yesterday, I took a photo that will become one of my favorite images of them. In it, they peek at me around oversized, saltwater-bleached roots formerly attached to a gargantuan tree, now a deformed-looking tangle, a wooden squid with severed tentacles. They have loved playing this form of peek-a-boo from behind deadwood and rock formations since they were very young. As much to my delight as theirs, they have not grown tired of it.

Now, sharing some amusement between themselves, they look a little bigger to me, like people on that fleeting cusp between childhood and young adulthood—growing, learning, and maturing, and yet still so fragilely and impressionably and hopefully young.

Years from now, they may not remember this moment. But I see something transpiring between them that burns a lasting impression on some deeper level, fusing the kind of bond that outlasts time and carries people through hardship.

To their left, the receding tide rolls small, quiet waves onto the beach, and the waves roll back again—posing no threat to us at the moment. But the Earth's first steady rhythm sounds a drumbeat of warning that we should heed; for whether in successful adaptation or worldwide catastrophe, the sea will unify us all.

Nate and Alex above Lake Ellen Wilson, Glacier National Park, Montana.

CHAPTER 6

THE BACKBONE
OF THE WORLD

AUGUST 2010

We hear the menacing snarls and let our eyes trace the sound to its source. Just a few hundred feet below where we stand at 7,050-foot Lincoln Pass in Montana's Glacier National Park, two grizzly bear cubs tussle playfully where this open, rocky mountainside meets a sparse conifer forest. Vigilantly close by, their mom vacuums her nose over the ground, searching for tidbits. A plus-size lady, she has a weight lifter's physique atop hips and legs that might cause a self-conscious bear to frown at her reflection in a lake. But she moves like a four-hundred-pound ballet dancer, hinting at speed and power that we cannot fathom.

Seeing her arouses a feeling so primal that few words even form in our minds or emerge from our mouths. Our skin prickles, our throats turn to sandpaper. If we possessed ears that normally drooped down, at this moment they would stand straight up. If we had the option, we would dive without further contemplation into a claustrophobic burrow and cower for a long time.

But we have no burrow. And the bears are just four or five steps off the trail we have to descend.

As any backpacker or armchair adventurer understands, this represents the worst possible circumstance. A grizzly bear alone might normally flee from the sounds and odors of humans, probably before the people even realized a bear lurked nearby. But other than a polar bear, a griz sow with cubs is arguably the most fearsome, ferocious terrestrial beast in the Americas. She may perceive any sizable creature in her vicinity as a threat to her babies. Every two or three years in the western U.S. or Canada, a sow horribly mauls or kills some hapless person guilty of no more than stumbling upon the same patch of earth at exactly the same moment as her cubs. In July 2011, a sow with cubs killed a 57-year-old man hiking with his wife in Yellowstone.

So we wait, hoping the bears will move on. There is no wind; they may not smell us. They disappear into the woods, but we periodically hear their growls, too close to the trail for us to consider venturing down there. An hour drips by like candle wax.

Three other hikers, two men and a woman, come along, heading in our direction. After a brief, lively huddle, we agree on a plan: we will walk in close formation down the trail, making abundant noise. Bears, according to conventional thinking, will not engage this large a group of people.

But apparently, these grizzlies did not read the rulebook.

As we buckle on backpacks, the woman says, gravely, "There are the bears." When we look downhill, she clarifies, "No, behind you."

We spin around. The sow, not thirty feet away, saunters noiselessly across the grassy meadow we're standing in, her cubs in tow. While we were strategizing how to outwit them with our superior intellects, they had pulled off a perfect flanking maneuver. From this close, we see her shoulder muscles rippling, the fur backlit by sunlight, and razor teeth designed for tearing through flesh as her mouth gapes open.

Then she sniffs the air and swings her head to stare directly at us.

IF THERE IS A national park that seems created to fulfill the grandest dreams of backpackers, it is Glacier.

Straddling the Continental Divide hard against the Canadian border, the northernmost U.S. Rockies resemble a collection of mountain-scale kitchen implements—meat-cleaver wedges of billion-year-old rock and stone knives lined up in rows that stretch for miles, everything standing with blades pointed upward. More than a hundred of them rise above eight thousand feet, the highest exceeding ten thousand feet.

Streams collect the runoff from fields of melting snow and ice, pouring down mountainsides, shouting loudest when crashing over innumerable cascades and waterfalls. Late-afternoon sunlight glints off pebbly creeks spilling from lakes, the water's surface sparkling like diamonds slowly twisting. Geological strata stripe mountainsides in parallel bands. Wildflowers in a palette of colors dapple vast, treeless tundra plateaus.

The Blackfoot called these mountains "the backbone of the world." The description fits a place where the land vaults up so dramatically from the very edge of the Plains—and where Triple Divide Peak is one of only two North American mountains that funnel waters to three oceans: the Atlantic, Pacific, and Arctic.

Swiss-born paleontologist Louis Agassiz, hailed as one of the greatest scientists of his time, comprehended the origins of places like the future Glacier National Park. In the 1840s, he theorized that an ice age had once locked up much of the planet. His ideas explained the signs of glaciers in Europe and North America where they did not exist: ground scraped down to striated bedrock, and massive "glacial-erratic" boulders deposited in meadows and forests by some mysterious but powerful force. Today, a glacier in the north of this park is named for him.

The renowned writer George Bird Grinnell, who began lobbying to designate the area a national park after visiting in the 1880s, called these mountains "the Crown of the Continent." The Great Northern Railway, hoping to bring in paying tourists, dubbed the area "Little Switzerland."

But in one important aspect, it differed from the Swiss Alps as much as Central Park from the Serengeti: unlike the settled Alpine valleys and mountainside meadows, the Northern Rockies were an intact, pristine wilderness. Today, some 90 percent of the park's million acres remain inaccessible except to those willing to explore on foot.

Glacier is among just a few U.S. wild lands outside of Alaska that host a nearly complete array of the continent's native megafauna. Only two are missing: the bison and woodland caribou. Sixty-two mammal species live here, and 260 kinds of birds are seen. Glacier and neighboring Waterton Lakes National Park in Canada have been designated an international peace park, an international biosphere reserve, and a World Heritage Site.

A backpacker on any of the park's more than seven hundred miles of trails may lose count of how many times she sees cliff-scaling, bearded mountain goats. Many backpackers go home with breathless tales of walking past that most regal of creatures, the bighorn sheep. Some—like my friend Geoff Sears when we took a trip here together—tell of leaving a sweaty T-shirt hanging outside to dry overnight, only to discover it even more soaked in the morning because deer have gummed it for the salt from perspiration. Hikers in early fall might hear bull elk bugle or see two bull moose clashing massive antlers.

Encounters with black or grizzly bears—both number in the hundreds here—occur rarely, for one simple reason: a bear will usually detect the humans first and avoid them. This dynamic undoubtedly serves the interests of both parties. A bear attacking people ultimately loses, as park officials will destroy it. And no one with a healthy attitude toward life wants to cross paths with a grizzly.

When Lewis and Clark explored the American West, the grizzly numbered an estimated 50,000 and ranged over two-thirds of the contiguous United States, from the Canadian border to Mexico to Ohio. While more numerous in Canada and Alaska, about 1,400 remain in the Lower 48, and they live only where humans tolerate them. More than seven hundred bears dwell in Glacier and the surrounding national forests, and another six hundred in Greater Yellowstone. Small, at-risk populations hang on in remote mountains in Washington, northern Idaho, and northwestern Montana.

No other species in North America shapes our perception of wilderness as definitively as the grizzly. There are wild lands with grizzlies, and there are those without, and they are as far apart in our minds as terror is from thrill.

Where they live, we enter the woods with a heightened alertness. Every dense copse of spruce trees or tall bushes potentially harbors a menace. Come upon a steaming pile of scat the size of a soccer ball, and you will wonder which direction the bear went and which you should go. We are not so far evolved from our hunter-gatherer ancestors to have lost our innate aversion to being eaten.

Encounter a great bear close up and, regardless of how you had planned to react, you may find yourself overwhelmed by one instinctive thought: flee. You backpedal, maybe stumble. You might reach for the pepper spray on your belt or forget it's there. You know in your bones that you possess little control over what happens next.

Terror hits hard right in the gut and takes the wind out of you. I know, because I've felt it.

When that sow grizzly and her cubs crept up so stealthily behind my friend Jerry Hapgood and me at Lincoln Pass on that late-summer morning, she not only Tasered us with one of the biggest, voice-seizing frights of our lives; she also clarified an unsettling truth: when you walk through country inhabited by grizzly bears, you see and hear them everywhere—except the ones that are actually right on top of you. To our good fortune and vast relief, that sow and her cubs merely continued on their way, giving us no more than a glance.

Now, eleven months later, I'm backpacking that same trail in Glacier with my wife and children, on another perfect summer day in mountains carved from glaciers but designed in dreams.

And I am thinking about bears.

"WHY CAN'T I CARRY a pepper spray?"

Nate badgers me persistently as we start down the Piegan Pass Trail, leaving behind a throng of camera-clicking, automobile-shackled tourists at Jackson Glacier Overlook on the Going-to-the-Sun Road. It is two o'clock. The sun smiles warmly from a cloudless blue dome. A breeze ripples through dry air. Get introduced to the Rocky Mountains on an idyllic afternoon like this one, and you will be in grave danger of uprooting your life and moving to some small Montana town at the edge of paradise.

My family is heading out for a much less binding adventure: a three-day backpacking trip to Gunsight Pass in Glacier—and views of the largest of this park's disappearing rivers of ice. And my son is preoccupied with the conviction that he should be armed with one of the pepper-spray canisters now holstered to the belts of Penny's and my backpacks.

I try reasoning with him—always a challenge with my hyperfocused nine-year-old. I explain that, as adults, his mother and I are better capable of responding to the very stressful circumstance of a charging bear. I don't admit that I'm not really sure I believe that. Instead, I resort to a parental fallback as old as spoken language: "Let's talk about it later, okay, buddy?"

After a short stop at Deadwood Falls, where the kids hurl sticks into water raging through a narrow gorge, the trail leads us up the gently rising, forested valley of the St. Mary River. Little more than a big stream here, the young river backs up in boggy flatlands, prime moose country, so we watch for them.

And we follow the protocols for hiking in grizzly country— staying close together and making noise so that bears will hear us from a distance and flee. We also walk with the kids sandwiched between me up front and Penny riding shotgun. I don't feel entirely sanguine about this strategy of sacrificing the old bull—me—to save the mother and our genetic investment. But there's no one to complain to about the arrangement.

Penny and I understand that bear attacks are rare. Still, we have a track record in Glacier that gives us pause.

Backpacking here seventeen years ago, the two of us stopped cold one afternoon, hearts suddenly slamming into our ribs. A hundred feet ahead, a bear stood silhouetted against a sunlit lake. Although it ran off, that image was burned into our minds. We returned in 2005, when Nate was four and Alex a two-year-old riding in a pack on my back. Day hiking popular trails, we missed, by minutes, a griz sprinting past paralyzed hikers on a trail so narrow they could barely lean out of its way. Two weeks after we took the kids up the Grinnell Glacier Trail, a man was badly mauled on it—but survived—while protecting his grown daughter from an attacking grizzly sow with cubs.

Besides, rational or not, it's hard not to imagine a bear eyeballing your kid as a relatively easy catch, and far more satisfying than another meal of huckleberries and whitebark pine nuts.

Three hours out, we traverse a mountainside of dense, chest-high brush. My eyes jump to every bush thrashing in the wind, every dark stump. But we probably have little to fear, given our noise level. Alex and Penny play a word game, Alex's chatter and window-shattering shrieks of laughter carrying on the wind. And for two solid hours of hiking, Nate hardly pauses for a breath while describing for me in exacting detail the myriad spacecraft he intends to design for a fleet needed to conquer the universe.

Where the trail crosses an open slope, we stop for a break. Below us, a thick shag of conifer forest rolls over the St. Mary Valley, ringed by mountains. I point out the Blackfoot and Jackson glaciers, explaining that, at one time, they were joined as one massive river of ice filling this valley. I tell Penny and the kids that the Blackfoot has alternately ranked as the largest and second-largest glacier in the park.

Nate and Alex glance up, then go back to their snack bars and to acting out their stuffed animals talking to each other. Even Penny has little to say. I look out at the glaciers again. The truth is, the view is beautiful, but the glaciers not so impressive. Melting has fragmented them into numerous lobes and fingers. It looks like milk rained on the mountains, leaving scattered white puddles.

In recent years, the Blackfoot has shrunk faster than computer models predicted it would. In the summer of 2007, a twenty-two-acre piece of it collapsed, releasing an avalanche of ice. Such major collapses indicate a glacier rapidly disintegrating, but this incident shocked scientists because they consider twenty-five acres the minimum threshold for calling something a glacier. In effect, an area the size of a small glacier disappeared almost instantaneously. "It just fell apart," one scientist told me.

BY SIX O'CLOCK, A bit over six miles and four hours from our car, we reach the backcountry camp at Gunsight Lake, claiming one of seven tent sites clustered in the forest near the lakeshore. Every other site is occupied by two to four backpackers; we have plenty of company. Above 5,000 feet, the sun feels like a hot-water bottle against our skin even late in the day. Tree-rustling exhalations of cool wind tumble down off mountains rising to 9,000 and 10,000 feet. Minutes after we arrive, the sun dips behind 9,162-foot Gunsight Mountain, and the air suddenly bites like October.

Nate corners me, a lobbyist buttonholing a key senator. I know which vote he wants to discuss.

So I demonstrate for my rapt kids how to discharge the pepper-spray canister. I slide the plastic safety clip off, hold the canister at arm's length aimed away, and show them the trigger without depressing it. They nod quietly when I emphasize they are not to touch one without permission, except in an emergency.

Then, to appease this persistent young man with whom I must hike and share a tent for the next couple of days, I let Nate carry one canister here in camp.

My son slides easily into the role of the world's only sixty-pound bodyguard. When I step out of the outhouse, he's waiting in a state-trooper pose, hands clasped behind his back, feet shoulder-width apart, face a mask of fearless resolve. Clipped to a belt loop in his pants, the pepper-spray canister looks like a mortar shell against his skinny thigh. "I'm here to escort you back to camp."

Following me around camp, he thinks out loud about future trips we're planning when he might carry pepper spray.

"What about Yellowstone? There are grizzlies there."

"We're going in January. They'll be asleep," I remind him.

"What about for alligators in the Everglades?"

"No one uses pepper spray on alligators. It's really only effective on animals with a strong sense of smell, like bears."

"Well," he informs me coolly, "when you're being dragged under-water by an alligator, you're going to wish you had listened to me."

Around nine o'clock, as dusk bleeds into darkness, I finish hanging our food in stuff sacks from a wire permanently strung high between two trees, beyond reach of bears. Nate stands sentry beside me, armed and more dangerous than I've considered. As we walk back to our tents, the loud crashing of an animal through the forest startles us.

Reaching for my pepper spray, I whirl toward the sound—and feel a rush of relief to see a deer in the dim light. Grinning, I turn back to Nate, thinking we'll share a laugh over being spooked by a deer. Instead, I find myself staring into the business end of a pepper-spray canister.

Nate stands with arms straight out, locked and loaded with me in his sights. I shudder to think how close he came to blasting me.

"See!" he burbles elatedly. "I was ready!"

Later, reading in the tent, I hear a huffing sound just outside our thin nylon walls. Nate sleeps beside me. Alex and Penny's tent stands just inches from ours. Penny announces flatly, "There's something snorting outside my tent." I understand her unspoken but implied directive: "See about that. I'll wait here."

I unzip my tent, slip on my boots, and step out into blackness. Scanning our campsite with my headlamp, I see only inky forest. I walk a short distance down the path, pepper spray in hand, shining my headlamp into the trees. A pair of eyes reflects the beam of light. Then I see the beast's outline: another deer.

As it turns out, several of them browse this campground day and night. They will clomp past our tents throughout our two nights here, not disturbing our slumbering kids but waking Penny and me repeatedly. It seems a revenge of sorts, for once the prey taunting the helpless predator.

Generations of hikers have walked the trails of Glacier National Park preoccupied by thoughts of an animal positioned higher up the food chain. Modern humans aren't used to wearing the silver medal in that contest.

But until scientific findings about global warming clarified in recent years, we were blind to a threat much larger than grizzly bears. The hardest danger to recognize is often the one we pose to ourselves.

IN 1850, SIXTY YEARS before becoming America's tenth national park, these mountains contained 150 glaciers covering thirty-eight square miles. It would be impossible for us to imagine today what this place looked like then, so different was it. Ice that had been in place for at least seven thousand years, fed by cold temperatures and abundant snowfall, extended deep into valleys and smothered mountainsides. Ice defined the landscape. It rendered much of the terrain barren and dictated what could live here and where.

Glaciers grow very slowly. Snow accumulates many feet deep through a mountain winter that ignores the calendar, commencing in autumn and not concluding until late spring. At higher, colder elevations, not all of the snow melts during the short summer. Snow crystals compress under their own weight into a transitional state called firn, and then gradually harden into dense ice. The ice—heavy, slick, and somewhat plastic—flows downhill. While a glacier's pace is far too torpid to observe with the eye, it does move faster on steeper slopes, forming crevasses where gravity stretches the ice like taffy.

At some point, the glacier descends to an elevation where more snow melts away in summer than accumulates in winter. This "equilibrium line," or "firn line," separates the glacier's higher "accumulation zone" from its lower "ablation zone." Here, the glacier is fed only from above, like a very long icicle, thick at its top even as water drips from its bottom.

Glaciers are born and die according to a simple and immutable physical process driven entirely by the long-term balance of snowfall versus melting rather than short-term weather patterns. This makes them a flawless barometer of climate shifts. Glaciers also hold clues to prehistoric climate. Snowflakes piling up trap tiny pockets of air, eventually entombing them in ice. Isotopes from ancient ice on Greenland and Antarctica reveal how atmospheric carbon dioxide levels have closely paralleled average temperature for hundreds of thousands of years. Glacial ice is to world climate what a canary was to early coal miners.

Unfortunately, in nature, entropy cares nothing for beauty or utility.

Around 1850, the three-century-long cold period known as the Little Ice Age came to an end and the climate started warming. As they did all over the world, glaciers in the Northern Rockies began to melt, imperceptibly at first, but then with more speed. When glaciers shrink, pulling backward uphill, they leave behind enormous trails of rubble called moraines—rock and dirt they had ground up and carried down the mountain while they were advancing. Like an arc of seaweed and shells deposited by a receding ocean wave, moraines show exactly how far a glacier once reached downhill.

As at Mount Rainier and other popular national parks, Glacier's complexion of a century ago has been captured in a trove of photographs taken by tourists, many now in the possession of park researchers. Some pictures show men and women in thick woolen suits and long dresses posing at the edge of ice as a hunter would stand proudly by the carcass of a slain bear—except that this bear is a white dragon, an inland sea of frozen water stretching to a far horizon. Other photos depict only the dragon. But where those old black-and-whites show ice, today there is dirt, rock, and traces of white.

The U.S. Geological Survey reports that Glacier National Park's average temperature has climbed by 2.1 degrees Fahrenheit over the past century—about twice the rate of warming worldwide. Of the 150 glaciers in the park a century and a half ago—the ice that carved these mountains into arrowheads and spear points—just twenty-seven remain. Glaciated area has declined from thirty-eight square miles to ten. More indicative of this demise, ice volume comprises a mere 10 percent of what once covered the park. Most glaciers today are small remnants, little more than glorified snowfields. The impacts of that diminished water resource trickle down to virtually every living thing in the park.

In 1887, when George Grinnell first laid eyes on the seven-hundred-acre glacier that would later bear his name, he described it as "a thousand feet high and several miles across." (His "thousand feet" measure no doubt referred to its elevation span, not the height of its snout, or ice cliff at its terminus.) Visited by hundreds of day hikers every summer, it has shrunk to about two hundred acres, losing a quarter of its area from 1993 to 2004 and another 9 percent between 2005 and 2007. In the summer of 2010, Grinnell Glacier suffered a large collapse, releasing so much ice into Grinnell Lake that, as one scientist told me, "You could almost walk across the lake on icebergs." The glacier "has retreated dramatically," he said. "Every time we go up there we're walking on rock that hasn't seen the light of day in four or five hundred years."

Pictures taken seventy years ago—when today's grandparents were children—show a sweeping fan of snow-covered ice filling a cirque. Today, an emerald lake covers much of the Grinnell's former area. There's a certain sadness in comparing a photo of Glacier taken decades ago to how it appears today, like watching a loved one who was once strong and proud falling into a sharp, terminal decline.

———

THE MOUNTAIN GOAT, AS white as a clean bed sheet, with straight horns that taper to ice-pick points, stares at us with coal-black eyes. We wait to see whether it will relinquish the trail to us, because there's no going around it. Penny, the kids, and I are day hiking from our camp on Gunsight Lake to Gunsight Pass, following a trail blasted in places out of sheer rock walls. To our left, steep slabs rise to soaring cliffs and a lobe of the Harrison Glacier, the park's largest, on Mount Jackson. To our right, the earth plunges over more cliffs a thousand feet down to Gunsight Lake, a deep-blue gourd squeezed between lushly green mountainsides below craggy peaks.

Alex turns her gaze from the goat thirty feet away to fix me with a look that says, "What's this animal going to do?" While I make no claims to insights on the thoughts of wild ungulates, it seems from this particular goat's expression that he's wondering the same thing.

After a calm standoff of a minute or two, the goat turns and scrambles nimbly down a rock face below the trail. We walk up to where it disappeared over the edge, but it's gone.

"Wow, I can't believe it went down there," Alex mutters. Moments later, it pops up thirty feet behind us, where we were just standing, and returns to browsing the few stunted plants growing here.

Mountain goats figure out what they need to do to get around trouble. We higher-evolved humans are not always so good at that—on many levels.

Far above the highest reach of the forest, beneath a blue sky sprayed by a few mare's tails of high, thin clouds, we look out over a great amphitheater of folded, uplifted walls painted in vivid stripes of red, ochre, gray, and white. Ribbonlike waterfalls pour hundreds of feet down them. Marmots whistle and sprint over steep tundra.

At wind-blasted Gunsight Pass, 6,900 feet above sea level, we sit on big, flat-topped rocks, perched on the rim of the high basin embracing Lake Ellen Wilson, where my friend Jerry and I camped a year ago. He and I encountered the grizzly sow and cubs a few miles beyond the lake, too far to reach today. After a lunch break, we turn around to retrace our hike up from Gunsight Lake.

Back in camp by midafternoon, Penny lies down with her book.

Nate and Alex change into sandals and lead me to the lake. As we walk through the campground's designated cooking area, where other back-packers sit around on logs, Nate shouts, "Oh my God, the deer are right there!" Then he announces, "One of them is trying to climb on the back of another one! I think he's trying to get a piggyback ride!"

At the lake, a breeze pushes little ripples toward us across a surface glinting in sunshine. While Alex and Nate wade in the shallow water, dropping stone bombs on stick ships, I lie back on sun-warmed beach pebbles, listening to my kids' laughter and screams and contemplating bombs of a different kind.

GLACIER HAS BECOME SOMETHING of a poster park for climate change, largely through the efforts of one man testifying to America about the consequences of our energy consumption.

Two decades ago, Dan Fagre accepted an offer to work in Glacier National Park without ever having been here—an easy decision for the longtime climber and backcountry skier who almost became an outdoor educator before science kidnapped him. Now in his late fifties, he runs the Glacier Field Station of the USGS Northern Rocky Mountain Science Center, leading a small team that hikes and skis into the mountains year-round to measure snow depth, tree distribution, soil moisture, and more. Using Glacier's dramatic story as a parable about climate change, he has given scores of interviews, and speaks at conferences around the world. In 2005, Fagre received the National Park Service Director's Award for Natural Resource Research.

Fagre and others told me their concern is not for the glaciers—that die has been cast—but for aquatic resources: stream flows, water temperature, what time of year snow melts, and the fallout for everything that relies on water, which is just about all of creation, including people. As elsewhere, precipitation increasingly falls as rain instead of snow. The winter snowpack melts out three weeks earlier than it did fifty years ago. The impacts ripple outward, leaving virtually no plant or animal species unaffected.

Fish such as bull trout that need cold water have stopped spawn-ing in two creeks surveyed, Bowman and Harrison. A tiny aquatic insect called the meltwater stonefly, or *Lednia tumana,* lives only in high streams chilled by melting glaciers. When the glaciers depart, *Lednia* "will be gone," Fagre said.

Considered an indicator of ecosystem health, the meltwater stonefly has been petitioned for listing under the U.S. Endangered Species Act. "This isn't just about an obscure insect that most people will never see—it's about an entire threatened ecosystem which harbors a whole suite of rare, poorly known, native species, the biology and survival of which are dependent on very cold water," said Joe Giersch, USGS scientist and coauthor of a 2011 study on alpine aquatic insects.

Didymosphenia geminata, also known as didymo or more descriptively as "rock snot," is a species of diatom that grows in warm, shallow water, coating stream and lake bottoms and choking off other species. A non-native, rock snot has recently been found in half of waters surveyed in the park.

The five-hundred-year-old stands of hundred-foot-tall western red cedar and western hemlock along Avalanche Creek, which offer a taste of the great forests of the Pacific Northwest, will be replaced in a hotter, drier climate by species like lodgepole pine, which may do well with more frequent, bigger blazes. The stand-replacing wildfires that burned a quarter million acres in the park in the 1990s and early 2000s, much of it old growth, were the most destructive in three centuries. Computer models show some forests being replaced by shrub- and grasslands.

At higher elevations, trees are invading tundra, which provides habitat for charismatic animals like mountain goats and bighorn sheep. Fagre has watched forest steadily cover a slope above Hidden Lake that, two decades ago, was almost entirely open.

Impacts on animals elude easy understanding because animals interact with their environments in complicated ways. Researchers have just a few pieces of a very large puzzle—they know, for instance, that wolverines den only in areas where snow persists into May. They are only beginning to assess the vulnerability of species like mountain goats, pikas, and Clark's nutcrackers.

"If you just look at glaciers for the past eight thousand years, or fires going back as far as we're able to go back, we're into new territory here in Glacier," Fagre told me.

The park's chief of science and resources management, Jack Potter, has worked here for forty years. Reflecting on the changes he has witnessed, he said, "You get used to a landscape that has green trees and abundant water resources, and these changes are rough. We've had whole forests that have become skeleton forests, like the whitebark pine where you see just bleached, dead trees," ravaged by mountain pine beetles that have thrived in warmer temperatures. "I expect you'll see [the changes] more pronounced in thirty or forty years."

"The glaciers are undoubtedly going to disappear," Fagre said. The increase in carbon dioxide, which lasts for decades in the atmosphere, already ensures a level of warming expected to eliminate the park's glacial ice by around 2020, though Fagre does not rule out the possibility of a few small, remnant ice patches hanging on a little longer.

Not everyone agrees with Fagre's timetable. Mauri Pelto, director of the North Cascades Glacier Climate Project and a professor of environmental science at Nichols College who's been studying glaciers since 1984, thinks some will linger at least until midcentury. He points to USGS findings that two of the park's largest, for instance, the Harrison and Rainbow, both covering roughly half of a square mile, each only lost about 9 percent of their area between 1966 and 2005. Most important, both still have a healthy accumulation zone. "If they've lost 10 percent of their area since 1966, why would you expect them to [shrink] five times as fast in the next decade?" Pelto said.

"Glaciers don't melt on schedule," Fagre told me. "But they're going to go soon."

BEFORE DARK ON OUR last evening, I walk to the lakeshore by myself, enjoying a moment of solitude that always, for me, makes the wilderness seem to expand as if injected with helium.

With no wind, the flat water reflects the mountains. Fish jump, creating expanding bull's-eye ripples. A waterfall across the lake plunges in three distinct steps of two or three hundred feet each. I notice a second ribbonlike fall beyond it, and eventually count seven within sight—so much water pouring down mountainsides, fed by reservoirs of melting snowfields above, nourishing green slopes below. The vestiges of a glacier that once filled this valley will feed these waterfalls for another decade or perhaps longer; after that, they will rely on another diminishing resource, snow.

In an August of my children's adulthood, someone standing here might see five waterfalls, or three, or two. That sight may still feel like a gift rather than a theft, but perhaps only if that person had not stood here years earlier and did not understand what had been lost.

I wanted my kids to see the park's dying glaciers. But as it turns out, while they may someday recall that the ice was the reason we came, it has not left much of an impression on them. I'm sure their enduring recollections will be of the mountain goat, the deer in camp, and playing in this lake.

Tomorrow, when rain falls for most of our four-hour hike out, soaking the trailside vegetation that brushes our legs, eventually soaking our pants and boots, Alex and Nate will glean a valuable lesson about hardship and patience. At one point, Alex will share with me her discovery of an eternal meteorological truism: "When I put my hood down, it starts raining, and when I put it up, it stops raining. So I'm going to put it up." And Nate will surprise me with this pearl from a nine-year-old's book of wisdom: "My body's miserable, and when my body's miserable I think of the hardest times I've ever had, and I feel better."

That knowledge may be worth more to them than seeing a withered glacier before it disappears.

Still, I can't help but wonder what we will have lost as a nation and a people when these glaciers are gone—this ice whose steady melting away is a starkly clarifying symbol of our excess. I wonder whether, through that loss, we will gain some self-knowledge and willingness to sacrifice for the generations to come—and what melting glaciers portend in terms of other challenges that later generations will face.

A million acres of wind, space, rock, sunshine, water, and nearly all of the animals that were intended for snowbound, midlatitude mountains in North America—that is Glacier in all of its anomalous perfection. As I have on past visits here, I feel the tidal insistence of time dragged forward at the imperceptible speed of geology, ice, epochs, and evolution, too slowly for our understanding to grasp.

But while watching my children play in Gunsight Lake, I also felt the competing tug of time passing at a human pace measured in pulses of the heart, in words and embraces, in moments here and suddenly gone. I know that, however long I live, there will be just one time in my life when Nate is nine years old and Alex is seven and I am sharing the beach on a lonely mountain lake in Glacier with them, laughing at hurled stones that send ripples with the impermanence of memories across clear waters, when we are still crackling with the electricity of having stood a few steps from a wild goat.

Epochs, days, moments—time is a dancer comfortable following any beat. We humans know only the metronome of lifetimes than rarely span a century, a period as fleeting as a microwaved meal on the planet's calendar. We venture forward somewhat uneasily into places like Glacier for awestruck glimpses of time's longer stride. Yet, we understand it only as well as we loosely grasp the breadth of the universe or the force of a prehistoric volcanic eruption recorded in layers of rock. But perhaps it's enough for us to know the emotions that places like Glacier inspire, that inflict us too infrequently: fear, wonder, and most of all, humility.

On very rare occasions, we stand at a convergence of differing paces of time—as I find myself now, with an odd sense of happy melancholy. For the children whose existence has taught me to measure time in the inexorable ticks of bedtime hugs and school years elapsed will only be young adults when ice that has witnessed millennia sees its time run out.

Nate, Jenna Berman, and Alex fishing in Ouzel Lake,
Rocky Mountain National Park, Colorado.

CHAPTER 7

IF A TREE FALLS

SEPTEMBER 2010

The flash of yellow at the edge of my peripheral vision grabs my attention as we walk up a trail through a shaded forest of mostly lodgepole pine. A small copse of several aspen trees stands in a column of sunlight against the dark backdrop of deep-green pines. Their leaves, golden with autumn, glow like a burning bush—ablaze without being consumed by their fire.

I point out the aspen to Nate and Alex, but they don't respond. They've had enough of being told what's pretty this summer. But that golden explosion is precisely one of the reasons I wanted to bring them here in the middle of September.

We're backpacking into the Wild Basin area of Colorado's Rocky Mountain National Park, on the east side of the Continental Divide and immediately south of the park's tallest and most famous mountain, 14,259-foot Longs Peak. Puffy white pillows drift lazily across a sky so blue it appears to have depth, like a lake. It may owe that hue to the elevation—we started hiking at 8,500 feet—and dry, clean air. But whatever the reason, I've rarely seen the sky that intensely blue outside the Rockies.

The afternoon temperature rests at about sixty-eight degrees, as if regulated with a thermometer. A gentle breeze stirs the air, like we're being fanned with giant palm leaves.

The Rocky Mountains in late summer are about as idyllic as the world gets.

A longtime friend, Bill Mistretta, who lives outside Denver, has joined us for this three-day hike. Years back, when I was child-free and we both lived in New England, we were frequent rock climbing partners. These days, it's a rare pleasure for us to get into the mountains together. As we walk, we reminisce and catch up on news about old friends. Bill, an engineer, can also talk science with my son for hours on the trail, debating earnestly while Nate expounds on his ideas for weapons of mass destruction that—in the interest of preserving the Earth—run on renewable energy sources.

More than providing good company, Bill is enabling our trip by carrying our stove, fuel, cook kit, and some food that did not fit into my overstuffed pack. Penny could not join us this time; she started a new job just a few weeks ago. Consequently, I'm hauling a load of gear and food even more onerous than usual—more than sixty pounds, or about 40 percent of my body weight—including a three-person tent instead of a two-person and most of our food for three days. I don't admit this to my kids, but I'm looking forward to taking a backpacking trip without them, just for the pleasure of walking without feeling like my hipbones are under a grinding wheel.

Apparently, I am not the only member of our party who feels overburdened.

We're just thirty minutes up the trail when Nate's little internal engine seizes up. "I'm dying!" he proclaims to the entire forest. "This pack is too heavy!" So we stop and, defying some immutable physical laws, I shoehorn his bag inside my pack. Heaving it onto my back again, I'm convinced it looks like I intend to dispose of a body in the woods.

But Nate's silent contentment and suddenly relaxed body language tells me that this is the correct strategy for us, today. We have many trail miles ahead of us to walk together, and the day will come when the bulk of our load has shifted from my back to his.

Nate's melodrama and my aches aside, neither of us is dying, of course. Suffering is relative, but if it tips too far out of balance, that's when things actually start dying.

———

IN 1999, IN THE pine forests blanketing mountains that rise as high as 13,000 feet above sea level just south of Rocky Mountain National Park, scientists first noticed mountain pine beetles accomplish something that none of their ancestors had for at least many decades: survive a Colorado winter in huge numbers.

A tiny, tree-boring insect the size of a grain of rice, the beetle typically lives for a year, laying eggs inside trees in summer. Normally, about 2 percent of those larvae emerge the following summer; most are killed by the sort of deep Arctic freeze common in the Rockies in winter.

But the winter of 1998–99 brought no such brutal cold snap. No one knows what percentage of mountain pine beetle larvae survived that winter; and not even the people who study pine beetles predicted what followed. But José Negrón, a research entomologist with the U.S. Forest Service Rocky Mountain Research Station, in Fort Collins, Colorado, recalls seeing unprecedented hordes of beetles that summer. "You could tell something was starting," he said.

Something was. Colorado stood at the brink of an outbreak that another Forest Service entomologist would dub "Beetlegeddon."

Mountain pine beetles, native to western North America, have gone through cyclical outbreaks at least for the century and a half of their recorded history, and research shows they have existed in western forests for thousands of years. But nothing known historically matches the scale of what happened in this century's first decade. Every new generation followed in the jointed-limb steps of its parents, reappearing every summer in a beetle baby boom that forest managers described as an epidemic.

In addition to milder winters skyrocketing the beetles' survival rates, a rare confluence of factors created what Negrón and other experts called a "perfect storm" for pine trees. A severe drought began in 1999 and continued for several years across the West, weakening trees. And in parts of Colorado and the West, there were numerous forests of lodgepole pine with trees older than eighty years. Lodgepole is a high-altitude species that dominates wherever it takes root—composing, for example,

almost eighty percent of Yellowstone's forest—and regenerates well after fires. These forests were uniformly older because they had replaced
stands logged or destroyed by wildfires in the late 1800s and early 1900s.

Big trees have more nutrients, meaning more beetles can live and
reproduce inside them. Many forests were filled with the large, mature
trees that mountain pine beetles consistently target for their mass attacks. As Negrón put it, "It made a nice banquet for the beetles."

The diminutive *Dendroctonus ponderosae*—*Dendroctonus* meaning
"tree killer" and *ponderosae* for "pine tree"—quickly gave new meaning to its Latin name.

The beetles swept across Colorado like a biblical plague, invading
350,000 acres of Colorado's Routt National Forest in 2007 alone. A survey found two-thirds of Rocky Mountain National Park's forests over-
run by bark beetles. In 2010, the Forest Service reported that mountain
pine beetles had infested 2.3 million acres in Colorado.

Colorado wasn't the first state to see a big outbreak of pine beetles—others had occurred in Montana's Glacier National Park in the
late 1980s and Idaho's Sawtooth Mountains in the mid-nineties. But
Colorado heralded the epidemic. Within a few short years in the new
millennium, the beetles mowed through Wyoming, Idaho, and Montana, spread east to the Black Hills of South Dakota, and migrated into
California and the Pacific Northwest. In British Columbia, by 2008,
more than 39 million acres of trees were dead, an area nearly the size
of Florida. The B.C. outbreak—ten times larger than anything previously known—began to subside only after most of the province's mature
lodgepoles had been killed.

The beetles have even ravaged pines—like whitebark, limber, and
bristlecone—that live at very high elevations, where it was historically
too cold for the insect. In some mountain ranges, more than half of the
whitebark pines are dead. Aerial surveys of Greater Yellowstone revealed
that 720,000 whitebark trees had been killed by beetles just in 2004.
The Forest Service reported in 2007 that whitebark "has disappeared
from as much as ninety-eight percent of its potential habitat in northern
Idaho."

Between 1999 and 2009, the mountain pine beetle killed billions of trees across more than 31 million acres of forest in the western United States. Include the area attacked by all native bark beetles—some of which target specific species, such as Douglas fir and spruce—and the affected area more than doubles, to 63 million acres, equal to the size of Oregon.

One official report after another invokes the grim phrase "landscape-level mortality." Some experts have described it as the largest forest blight ever seen in North America.

Because the beetles generally ignore young lodgepoles, those forests won't disappear; the trees still drop seeds to produce new trees. But the visible impact on the landscape will remain for two or three human generations, the time required for lodgepole to grow to maturity. Scientists, though, express much less optimism about the fate of higher-elevation trees, like the majestic whitebark pine.

Besides the tragic sight of millions of acres of green turned rust-red, the beetle epidemic has commanded the attention of scientists and public-lands managers for an even more troubling reason: these natural disasters are magnified by the hotter, drier summers and milder winters that scientists say have arrived across the West and will intensify in tandem with rising atmospheric carbon levels. At Grand Lake, near the town of Frazier, Colorado, daily low winter temperatures regularly averaged below zero Fahrenheit before 1975, according to weather station records dating to 1939. But no winter since 1975 has seen average lows below zero, and the temperature graph has trended steadily upward. At Loch Vale in Rocky Mountain National Park, the average year-round temperature leaped 3.5 degrees just from 1984 to 2007.

The tiny mountain pine beetle—the largest of several blights afflicting America's trees—may portend what lies in store for our great forests.

CHILDREN MAY NOT WREAK havoc on a level comparable to beetles, but they have one thing in common: both can sense when you are short-handed and vulnerable.

Although Bill's load-bearing assistance is indispensable, it's outside his job description to assist with my hardest task: crowd control. Not having Penny along leaves me as lone keeper of law and order for my kids—a miserable assignment. And children know that a parent flying solo teeters on the edge of cracking. So they are less inhibited with their complaints, bolder in their defiance, and more brazen in their battles with each other. On the drive up here in Bill's truck, out of the corner of my eye, I saw a flash of flying hands in the back seat as they quietly pummeled each other, figuring I would not notice.

Bill observes all of this mutely, like the childless fortysomething that he is—figuratively wiping his brow, as if he's dodged a bullet. I knew that feeling until I was almost forty. Then I had kids. I'm still waiting for my Parenting Purple Heart.

But as we ascend the trail through shady pine forest, passing boulders the size of dump trucks—deposited by a long-gone glacier—Alex and Nate forget their differences. These trips always motivate my kids to reach a truce, realizing they represent each other's main source of entertainment for days to come.

Two hours, three miles, and a thousand feet uphill from the trailhead, we turn onto a narrower footpath at a sign that reads "Siskin," marking our campsite for the night. It leads to a clearing in the pines that is ours alone, furnished with abundant, big rocks and logs to sit and cook on.

Nate and Alex swap boots for sandals and trot down to the creek that's flowing swiftly, but also safely shallow, less than a hundred feet below the main trail. They spend the next ninety minutes playing there, granting me a much-needed reprieve from emotional effort in our quiet space amid the lodgepoles. Bill and I unload packs, pitch tents, lay out bags and pads, and get water. Then we recline on a couple of flat-topped boulders, recalling that, three years ago, we carried a few cans of beer to our high camp on Mount Rainier. We wouldn't mind having those right now.

Nearby, another copse of golden aspen catches fire just before the sun sets behind a hilltop in early evening. Then the temperature abruptly spirals south.

AROUND THE SAME TIME as Colorado's pine beetle outbreak, another, more mysterious blight turned up in a tree that intermingles with lodgepole pine at five thousand to eight thousand feet in the Rockies—a tree that, in many ways, embodies Colorado flora: the aspen.

Thanks to a flattened stem that grows perpendicular to each leaf, aspen leaves tremble in a breeze like thousands of fluttering bird wings—the reason the tree is also called "quaking aspen." This trait is actually an adaptation that maximizes photosynthesis in the short growing season at high elevations. But to a human eye, those vibrating aspen groves transform a landscape from still life to theater. Unlike the dull brown of many tree species, the fresh-scrubbed look of aspen's cream-colored bark brightens a mountainside. And with its brilliantly golden coloration in autumn, the aspen represents the rejoinder of the Rocky Mountains to my native New England's spectacular fall foliage.

A significant part of Colorado's $7 billion tourism industry, which supports 200,000 jobs, depends on those golden leaves.

So people noticed when, in the summer of 2004, in southwestern Colorado, aspen got sick: leaves began turning brown, branch tips died, and trunks blistered. The following year, the trees failed to leaf out. The blight—soon given the emotive acronym SAD, for Sudden Aspen Decline—spread aggressively around the state, afflicting more than half a million acres by 2008, almost one-fifth of Colorado's aspen. The heaviest devastation occurred in western Colorado, where the tree is more abundant.

Aspen thrives on catastrophic disturbances, often (though not always) sprouting up opportunistically in the wake of a wildfire, avalanche, or logging. For that reason, ecologists call it an "early successional" or "pioneer" species. The tree reproduces by dispersing seeds on the wind and by cloning itself through an extensive root system. An entire hillside of aspen can be interconnected underground and genetically identical.

The SAD plague has differed from past changes in aspen patterns in its speed and breadth—occurring within a few years rather than over decades, and affecting landscapes rather than single stands. Normally, while individual trees live not much longer than a century, new clones keep repopulating healthy stands as older trees die. But much about the aspen's environment fell out of balance at the same time.

While SAD eliminated mature trees, especially on southern and western slopes at lower altitudes, browsing by cattle and elk has inhibited the regeneration of seedlings. As with the mountain pine beetle, experts say SAD was aggravated by the drought, making aspen vulnerable to attacks by pests like cytospora cankers and poplar borers. In 2002, Colorado saw the lowest precipitation—sixty percent of its long-term average rain- and snowfall—and highest summer temperatures of any year from 1950 to 2006, conditions that were "more severe for aspen than in any other year" during that period, according to a November 2009 article in the journal *Forest Ecology and Management.*

By 2009, SAD had swept through Utah, Nevada, and parts of Arizona and Wyoming. Some researchers were suggesting that a third of Colorado's aspen could be dead within a few years. A U.S. Forest Service report in 2010 noted that the spread of SAD had slowed or stopped, and while the damage was "severe and unprecedented," and some stands will disappear, "most affected areas had some aspen regeneration."

The future of aspen remains cloudy. Some researchers told me that aspen's recovery may depend largely on the extent to which young sprouts survive browsing by elk, which can nibble an aspen grove to death, a major problem on the east side of Rocky Mountain National Park and elsewhere (largely attributed to the lack of predators such as wolves to control elk numbers). At any rate, it takes fifty years or more for aspen to reach full height. Areas hard hit by SAD won't return to "normal" for at least a half century, given a return to more favorable conditions.

But that is unlikely. The *Forest Ecology and Management* article predicted that, by 2060, 76 percent of aspen groves hit by SAD will no longer have a climate hospitable to the tree. That study was based on a computer model that examines landscapes on a large scale, so it does not account for small-scale influences that could affect aspen for better or worse. But it concludes: "Aspen, in fact, may be a prime indicator of the impacts of a changing climate on forest growth and productivity as the balance between temperature and precipitation becomes less and less favorable."

As it turns out, the SAD and mountain pine beetle outbreaks may be merely acute symptoms of a larger, more chronic affliction in western forests.

A January 2009 article in the journal *Science* reported that "tree death rates have more than doubled over the last few decades in old-growth forests of the western United States." Describing the trend as "pervasive," the article noted that the spiked death rate has occurred across a wide range of forest types, at all elevations, in trees of all sizes and species: pines, hemlocks, firs, and others. It warned of the potential for "cascading effects," including ecosystem shifts that render forests unsuitable for the birds and animals that depend on them for food and habitat.

That study, led by U.S. Geological Survey scientists, concluded that "the most probable cause of the worrisome trend is regional warming." And it pointed out the multiplying impact: dying forests stop functioning as carbon "sinks," removing carbon dioxide from the atmosphere; they become carbon sources, releasing CO_2 as trees decompose—more quickly when burned—and "further speeding up the pace of global warming."

No one can predict the next pine beetle or SAD epidemic or other, new tree blight. But warming is tipping the natural balance of things in favor of disease and insects over trees.

"WHEN ARE WE GOING to stop? When are we going to find some shade?"

Alex bombards me with questions intended to convey her general dissatisfaction with our circumstances. On our second day in Rocky Mountain, we're about an hour into a relatively easy, three-mile hike from Siskin camp to our next campsite, at Ouzel Lake. My kids have walked three times this distance on several occasions. Today, I'm getting some serious blowback.

We've left the cool shade of the lodgepole forest, following the trail up onto a broad, open ridge, an ancient glacial moraine separating the valleys of Ouzel Creek and North St. Vrain Creek. Burned in 1978, the terrain illustrates how wildfire spawns new life. Lodgepole pine and aspen saplings with yellow leaves spring up from the grassy earth among blackened, dead trunks. Lodgepole pine has evolved to need fire. Its cones are sealed by a resin that is broken to release seeds only in temperatures between 113 and 140 degrees Fahrenheit. Such temperatures are produced in nature by only one phenomenon: fire.

Ahead of us, a wall of snowy, craggy mountains, including Longs, stretches around half of our horizon. But there's hardly a patch of shade bigger than a nickel along this trail. Despite a pleasant breeze and a temperature around 70 degrees Fahrenheit, the high-altitude sun is making us feel like pancake batter plopped onto a hot griddle. I've promised Nate and Alex that we'd stop for a snack at the next cool spot, and they're getting annoyed that I cannot conjure shade from the scorched earth.

A day hiker walking in the other direction beams at our scene of familial bonding in nature and says, "Looks like a great trip!" I force a smile. After he passes by, Nate mutters, "We'd better stop soon or I'm going to die of heatstroke."

Finally, I give up on finding any substantial shade, instead parking the kids in the fingerlike shadow of a lone, burned-out snag, and piling snacks in front of them. Then I walk away under the pretense of going to pee, but really to escape their complaining.

After several therapeutic minutes of standing by myself, with no one proposing to crucify me for some minor offense like not bringing pepperoni, I return to find my children have undergone a miraculous personality change. I'm consistently amazed over the social good accomplished by pouring food into small bodies. Nate and Alex stand and put on their packs without a negative word, and soon we're bouncing along, laughing together over some silliness.

Less than an hour later, I drop my pack—cursing it under my breath—onto the hard-packed dirt of the only campsite at Ouzel Lake, a minute's walk from the lakeshore and just seconds from the lake's outlet creek. There's plenty of space for Bill's tent once he arrives later this afternoon; he hiked out to the trailhead this morning to meet his girlfriend, who's driving up from Denver to hike in and camp with us tonight. At just over 10,000 feet—the highest point we will reach on this year of park adventures—the lodgepole-ringed lake sits below that wall of 12,000- and 13,000-foot peaks we looked up at walking in here: Copeland, Ouzel, Mahana, Isolation.

We have this piece of subalpine paradise entirely to ourselves.

Alex and Nate dart toward the lakeshore. I promise to join them eventually. But first, with my hip flexors killing me, my soles throbbing, and my lower back reduced to a state of semipermanent knothood, I lay out a sleeping pad on the ground in the shade of some pines.

Lying on my back, I gaze up at wispy mare's-tail clouds and the pine trees encircling our campsite, the tallest maybe forty feet high, all of them straight and thin with stubby branches. The wind follows a pattern I've heard in mountain cirques like this one many times: each gust starts high above us, barely audible from a distance but building in volume as it barrels downhill. A long, expectant minute later, the gust roars through camp like a speeding train, stirring up a tornado of dust and leaves. After a moment of quiet, I hear the next wind train begin at the mountaintops. It will come like that again and again until evening.

Watching the trees sway, I notice branches here and there with red, dead needles. Wild Basin hasn't been hammered by beetles yet; its lodgepole pines do not have the widespread rusty discoloration seen in heavily hit areas. But no one I spoke with doubts they will invade.

It occurs to me that more of this basin—including this campsite—could become like that hot, exposed burn area we passed through on the hike in, as an increasing number of dead trees become fuel for the next big conflagration.

MOUNTAIN PINE BEETLES KILL trees in a death by many thousands of cuts. Using sophisticated chemoreceptors to identify host trees, they descend on entire forests of pines. The trees sprout thousands of "pitch tubes," small white, pink, or brown blobs of resin where female beetles bore through the bark into the phloem, the layer that transports nutrients and water through a tree. The females release a pheromone that draws males into the tree, where each beetle pair produces up to seventy-five eggs. Very quickly, beetles and larvae girdle the tree's insides. The beetles carry spores of blue stain fungi that also reproduce. Together, beetles and fungi starve a tree by cutting off its vascular system.

Within five to ten days, the tree is dead. Nothing can save it. Within a year or two, its needles turn red and fall to the ground. The summer after an attack, enough new beetles emerge from each dead tree to kill at least two more trees.

Beetle larvae insulate themselves in winter by metabolizing a glycerol that works like antifreeze; it takes at least five consecutive days of temperatures thirty degrees below zero Fahrenheit or colder to kill them. Now, in some parts of Colorado and elsewhere above 9,500 feet, warmer winters have allowed mountain pine beetles to produce a new generation annually instead of every two to three years, as they had done historically. That reproductive leap magnified the outbreaks two- and three-fold, Barbara Bentz told me.

"We're seeing the results of climate change now in high-elevation places," Bentz, a research entomologist with the U.S. Forest Service Rocky Mountain Research Station in Logan, Utah, said. In a 2010 article in the journal *BioScience,* Bentz and her coauthors predicted that the forests of western North America will see increasing outbreaks of spruce and mountain pine beetles in coming decades.

Some tree species will fare well. Ponderosa and lodgepole pine are adaptable and will likely continue to grow widely across the West. As Dan Binkley, professor of forest ecology at Warner College of Natural Resources in Fort Collins, Colorado, told me, "Most of the old trees in almost all of Colorado's lodgepole pine forests" have been killed. But "we still have millions of healthy young lodgepoles."

Many species, however, will not do so well. Studies suggest that some will shift their range northward by hundreds of miles in this century. But many cannot migrate north or uphill. And the death of entire stands of whitebark pine raises the specter of some species disappearing in a warmer climate with more pine beetles.

From the Rockies to the Cascades and High Sierra, the whitebark pine has long been a symbol of tenacity with its twisted trunk and gnarled bark, sometimes leaning away from prevailing winds. Whitebark pines exist at the highest elevations that trees grow in the West, up to 11,000 feet in the Rockies and 12,000 feet in the southern Sierra. They live an average of about eight hundred years, with the oldest known, in central Idaho, nearly 1,300 years old. *Pinus albicaulis* produces a small seed that's high in fat and provides an important food source for more than a hundred animal species, from Clark's nutcrackers to grizzly bears.

White pine blister rust, a disease inadvertently imported from Asia a century ago, now infects whitebark pines nearly throughout their range. It invaded the Northern Rockies seventy to a hundred years ago—which represents basically one whitebark generation, not nearly enough time to develop adaptations. There, 80 percent of trees are infected. In the past ten years, the disease has migrated south into Colorado and New Mexico. In a 2007 report, Professor Diana Tomback of the University of Colorado at Denver wrote, "Blister rust alone has the potential to cause local, if not regional and even range-wide extirpation of white-bark pine."

Now, the mountain pine beetle—buoyed by a warming climate— poses an even greater threat to the continued survival of whitebark. Limber pines at high elevations in Rocky Mountain National Park and elsewhere face the same threat. So do bristlecone pines, which grow at elevations as high as 11,000 feet in Great Basin National Park and in mountain ranges from Utah to California. The oldest bristlecone, named Methuselah, is more than 4,800 years old. Its location in the White Mountains of east-central California is kept secret to protect it.

As a 2006 study led by Gerald Rehfeldt, a plant geneticist with the Rocky Mountain Research Station in Moscow, Idaho, noted, "By the end of the century, about forty-eight percent of the western U.S. landscape is predicted to experience climate profiles with no contemporary analog to the current coniferous vegetation." It's a lot to ask of plants to endure in an environment they have never experienced before. Animals, too, for that matter. Including humans.

While interviewing experts on trees and beetles, I was told repeatedly, "You have to speak with Bill Romme."

Romme, a professor of forestry at Colorado State University, has spent forty years examining everything from the 1988 Yellowstone fires to the recent pine beetle epidemic. He told me, "I think we can't begin to understand what's going in the forests until we understand what's happening with climate."

He unequivocally links beetle outbreaks, SAD, and increasing wild-fires to droughts and warming temperatures. He's bullish on the future for lodgepole pine, but thinks aspen habitat will shrink. As for white-bark pine, a species he affectionately calls "a really cool tree," Romme said the future "is kind of grim, actually."

He suspects that whitebark will survive "in very small numbers throughout most of its current range." But it may disappear from warmer, drier areas as temperatures continue climbing. He echoes other researchers' concern that the multiple stresses on whitebark and the Clark's nutcracker and red squirrels that distribute its seeds may eventually mean fewer and fewer seeds, spelling the tree's doom. In Colorado, which does not have whitebark but hosts its high-elevation analog, limber pine, Romme anticipates "a tremendous reduction in the number of limber pine at tree line."

As for what Wild Basin's future holds, Romme said, "it really depends on how rapidly the climate changes. But within the next forty years, we will almost certainly see a large fire in that area."

Then Bill Romme digressed from science into sentiment.

"I really love these forests—that's why I've spent my life in them," he said. "If climate change is going to be as bad as projected at the end of this century, I think all bets are off. I also hate to see the loss of the whitebark pine, because it's a beautiful tree and it's dying not for natural reasons but because of what we're doing to the climate."

After a pause, he added, "For all those reasons, I kind of cry when I see the whitebark pine forests."

As I'm reading a book in the afternoon shade of the lodgepoles at our campsite, Alex wanders up to lie down beside me with her book, leaving Nate contentedly working on his dams on the creek. My daughter reads as many hours a day as the average American kid sits in front of an electronic screen. She and I are constantly challenging our local children's librarian to find chapter books that Alex hasn't already read five times.

We exchange smiles and winks as she lies against my side and fixes an intent gaze on her book. It mimics our evening ritual at home, reading side by side on the couch. Every night, too, I carry her piggyback to bed, with her "steering" me into walls en route to her room, where I pretend to fall asleep in her bed. Then we share our secret handshake and blow each other a kiss as I walk out her door. We maintain this routine when camping, with me carrying her to the tent at night.

I think I'm going to painfully miss this stage in her life once it passes.

By midafternoon, Bill hikes into camp with his girlfriend, Jenna Berman, an athletically built, outgoing woman in her thirties who works for a bicycling-advocacy organization in Denver. Jenna casually pulls out her fly-fishing rod and offers Nate and Alex a lesson. They go to her like ants to spilled honey.

When Nate selects a fly, she tells him, "Great choice, good color." She and the kids wade thigh-deep into the lake, with Jenna first demonstrating then letting each of them practice casting. Then they head for the creek and Jenna immediately points at a calm pool. "See in front of that rock? There's a cutthroat in there. He's chillin'," she tells them. Nate makes a few casts, the fish bites, and Jenna helps him reel it in. But as he's holding the net, the trout leaps from Jenna's hands back into the creek—prompting a blast of laughter from the kids.

They spend the rest of the afternoon and early evening fishing the creek. In the tent later, Nate makes me promise we'll take up fly-fishing together.

What began as a seemingly disastrous trip has morphed into one that Nate and Alex will remember as one of their favorites. It's another reminder for me that children possess incredible plasticity: presented with something that cheers them, they will instantly forget their misery of a moment earlier. Look hard enough and one can find redeeming aspects in almost any situation—emphasis on *almost*.

So it is with the story of the western forests. The lodgepole pine has adapted to ten thousand years of wildfires and beetles; it has achieved a working balance and will persevere. But it's hard to find consolation in that fact while writing the epitaph for whitebark, limber, or bristlecone pines—or at best, seeing the ranges of trees that symbolize perseverance shrink to museum stands in a few last strongholds.

On our final morning, another clear, calm, late-summer Rocky Mountains day is born in freezing temperatures, but quickly warms to T-shirt-and-shorts weather. After fishing the creek more, we start the five-mile downhill hike back to the cars. Less than a mile from Ouzel Lake, we run into friends Jon and Heather Dorn and their daughters Hadley, who's fourteen, and Abby, who's twelve; they knew we were up here and hiked in this morning to join us for the walk out.

Along St. Vrain Creek, in the cool shade of tall lodgepoles, Jenna casts into eddies and pools. All four kids crowd around her, watching with animated expressions—not the blank faces of children glued to a television. Jenna reels in a brook trout. As she cradles it gingerly in her hands, Alex, Nate, Abby, and Hadley rub their fingers on its slick body.

Then Jenna bends down and, in a small gesture of balance, releases the trout back into the wild creek, where it flicks its tail and is gone.

Joshua trees at Joshua Tree National Park, California.

CHAPTER 8

SEARCHING FOR DR. SEUSS

NOVEMBER 2010

After our plane touches down and rolls to a stop at the gate, a flight attendant announces over the intercom to the passengers, who are over-represented by families with young children, "Welcome to John Wayne-Orange County Airport, the airport also known as Disneyland."

Alex and Nate shoot excited looks at Penny and me. In their minds, all this talk of camping and rock climbing at Joshua Tree National Park was very possibly a clever ruse we concocted to cover up a surprise vacation to Southern California's much more famous park. Like any kids their age, they still believe in miracles.

Penny and I shoot each other "uh-oh" looks, fearing mutiny, then turn back to the kids. We smile and shrug. It seems a pathetic response, but then, we weren't prepared for a flight attendant announcing to every kid on the plane that they were going to Disneyland.

To our surprise, though, Nate and Alex grin right back at us—somehow amused by this. I'm not sure what this says about us as parents, but our kids appear to accept that our family is different from the others. Still, as we're driving to Joshua Tree, Nate feels compelled to state his objection for the record.

"How come you had to go to a park that's close to Disneyland?" he says to me. "I like camping and all that, but I don't want to be *near* Disneyland and *not go to* Disneyland!"

The episode seems a valuable first lesson for my kids in a truism they are likely to encounter again: in Southern California, things are not always what they appear to be.

Penny and I first visited Joshua Tree to rock climb eighteen years ago, long before marriage and kids, and the year before the place was upgraded from a national monument to a national park. Coming here always conjures descriptors like "another universe" in my mind—and that impression usually sets in long before we reach the park.

Like invasive weeds, the sprawl of asphalt, subdivisions, and strip malls follows Interstate 10 more than a hundred miles east into the Southern California desert, halting abruptly at the boundary of Joshua Tree National Park. There, instead of buildings, scores of rock formations rise two hundred feet or more above the high-desert plateau. Rock climbers pepper the cliffs. For decades, this park has been one of the sport's great meccas. There are hundreds of named rock formations and thousands of climbing routes.

Driving through the park, I immediately recognize many formations I've climbed and am gripped by the feeling of reuniting with an old friend I haven't seen in a long time, but who hasn't changed a bit. Though years have passed, the same fevered anticipation accelerates my pulse when I'm surrounded by so much golden granite and planning to get on it.

Under a warm sun in Ryan Campground, Penny sets off on a short hike and Nate and Alex take off to explore the broad, chunky rock formation standing at least fifty feet tall and three times as wide right behind our campsite, which they've already christened "the kid fort." Giving them the most-ignored piece of advice in human history—"Be careful"—I unload the car and pitch our tent.

A black-tailed jackrabbit bounds away, startled by our noise. Desert spiny lizards zip over boulders; cactus wren flit among the bushes and cacti. A memory flashes back across eighteen years of Penny and me sitting in the calm chill of a December evening, after a full day of climbing here, when a coyote materialized from the pitch darkness and sauntered casually past without even a glance at us.

Within minutes, the kids call down from a wide ledge near the top of the rock formation: "Dad, come up here!" I scramble up, partly to let them give me a tour, partly to delineate for them where they are permitted to venture and which areas I consider unsafe. Those boundaries will become as disputed as Kashmir's over the next three days as Nate and Alex lobby for more freedom.

Babbling effusively, they lead me over boulders and up steep slabs, across ledges and through a narrow, sandy-bottomed corridor between two granite walls. Using a twenty-foot length of thin utility cord I've given them, they lower their stuffed animals down short cliffs. As much as I've climbed here, I had never before fully appreciated Joshua Tree's infinite value as a vast jungle gym. Barely an hour after our arrival, Alex suggests to me, "We should come back here for spring break so we can stay for a week." I could almost weep.

Despite the summerlike temperatures, the November days are short. The sun sets before six o'clock. As bands of yellow, orange, and red backlight the Little San Bernardino Mountains several miles to the west, I gaze at the Joshua trees fanning out across the flat pan of desert. Most rise no taller than fifteen or twenty feet. Rarely do any two stand within ten feet of each other, as if they require a lot of personal space. This sparse assemblage does not call to mind any conventional image of a "forest."

And yet, they dominate the landscape through their sheer numbers and arresting exoticism. Thousands of Joshua trees march toward every distant horizon. On most, twisted branches sprout atop a thick, straight, fibrous trunk. The branches terminate in headlike, tight clusters of foot-long evergreen "leaves" whose dagger shape no child would sketch when asked to draw a leaf. Others lack branches, the floral impersonation of a fence post. They seem most eerie now, at dusk, like zombies staggering across the desert in a B movie.

The Joshua resembles both a tree and a cactus and yet neither—a crossbreed between the two that appears unfinished, missing vital parts that would give us visual clarification of its identity. It looks like something fictional sprung from a vivid imagination, which is probably why so many observers have drawn comparisons between the Joshua and the delightfully unreal vegetation depicted in the books of Dr. Seuss.

I'm hoping Nate and Alex—longtime fans of the doctor—see the same parallel.

In a sense, the Joshua tree fits right into the other-universe weirdness of Southern California. It is SoCal's ur-oddball, predating by several millennia the oddities of human culture. Even in a biologically rich environment of 813 species of vascular plants, many of them bizarre, the Joshua tree ranks among the most charmingly peculiar. And even competing with these amazing granite monoliths, it earns top billing in the park's name.

Which just makes the outlook for my old friend Joshua Tree National Park feel that much more tragic.

THE JOSHUA TREE, FIRST identified as *Yucca brevifolia* by the eminent German-American botanist George Engelmann in 1871, populates an impressive sweep of the desert Southwest. Its range spans 25,000 square miles across Southern California, southern Nevada, northwestern Arizona, and southeastern Utah, an area larger than West Virginia. The tree's habitat is defined by the Mojave Desert—or rather, the Joshua tree defines the Mojave's boundaries because it's considered an indicator species for the desert: it grows nowhere else in the world. Not actually a tree but a giant yucca that in rare instances reaches more than forty feet tall, the Joshua thrives in grasslands such as the Queen Valley and Lost Horse Valley of its namesake park.

Like many plant species, it owes its considerable reproductive success to a decidedly unromantic bodily function: the bowel movement.

Many birds and animals, from rodents to bears, assist the reproduction of plants by eating their seeds and later dropping them, swathed in nature's fertilizer, in some other location. Producing seeds that are palatable and nutritious to a variety of fauna is a primary mechanism by which plants "migrate" to expand or shift their range with long-term fluctuations in climate.

But the Joshua tree is unusual in that one megafauna species was largely responsible for its huge distribution: the Shasta ground sloth. Researchers have found fossilized remains of sloth dung bursting with whole seeds, fruit, and other parts of Joshua trees. In fact, the Joshua's seed pods do not break apart and release seeds as smaller plants' do. Like those of only a few other large yuccas, these pods appear to be adapted to dispersal by giant prehistoric herbivores.

Unfortunately for the Joshua, the Shasta ground sloth went extinct in North America almost 13,000 years ago. Since then, no large, highly mobile animal has offered Joshua seeds the free ride through prodigious dung dispersal that they formerly received from the sloth. The tree has relied on seed-caching rodents like pack rats and ground squirrels, which are capable of breaking open its pods to distribute its genetic material. But rodents don't travel far and wide like the long-departed sloth.

Mormon settlers crossing the Mojave Desert in the mid-nineteenth century purportedly named the tree for the Biblical character because they saw the tree, like Joshua, raising its arms, gesturing them toward the Promised Land. Around the same time as the Mormons, ranchers and gold miners infiltrated the high desert, using the tree's trunk and limbs for fence posts and corrals and burning the wood in steam engines that processed ore. Long before them, Native Americans used the Joshua's tough leaves for baskets and sandals and ate the flower buds and seeds.

Yucca brevifolia has adapted exceedingly well to a region that receives just three to ten inches of rain a year, and where summer temperatures routinely top 100 degrees Fahrenheit. The trees grow widely spaced so that their extensive root systems can soak up water from infrequent rainstorms before it evaporates. Seeds require rain to germinate, and seedlings may grow three inches per year for the first ten years—but then slow way down. Unlike true trees, Joshuas do not have growth rings; researchers estimate their age based on a long-term average annual growth rate of a half inch.

Freezing winter temperatures spur Joshua trees to flower, which leads to branch growth. The yucca moth pollinates Joshua flowers, simultaneously laying eggs in the flower ovary; the eggs hatch into larvae, and the larvae survive on Joshua seeds in classic symbiosis. From February through April, the trees bloom with showy, cream-colored flowers packed tightly together in enormous clusters bigger than a watermelon.

But the park's Joshua trees are sick. Rising average temperatures and severe droughts appear to be killing them off. And it's going to get hotter. Climate models forecast that the Southwest deserts will see some of the greatest departures from current climatic conditions in all of temperate North America, with temperatures leaping by up to six to seven degrees Fahrenheit in this century.

In findings announced in March 2011, U.S. Geological Survey research ecologist Ken Cole and a team from Northern Arizona University, the National Oceanic and Atmospheric Administration, the University of Arizona, Lawrence Livermore National Laboratory, and the U.S. Forest Service's Rocky Mountain Research Station predicted that the Joshua tree will no longer survive in 90 percent of its current range within sixty to ninety years. It will hang on only in pocket refuges at the northern end of its range, miles from Joshua Tree National Park.

Very possibly within the lifetimes of my children, this iconic giant yucca will disappear from the park named for it. After that, as with the fictional trees of Dr. Seuss, visitors will see it only in photos and the pages of books.

"DAD, FOLLOW ME THROUGH here."

Nate beckons to me, then turns and squirms into a narrow crack between two boulders on "the kid fort." I peer inside. He worms through a passage that does not look wide enough for my head to pass through cleanly, never mind my torso. It continues for fifteen feet or more to its other end, where sunlight enters through a vertical mail slot of an opening.

Having visions of my ribs or skull getting jammed in there, I decline his invitation to follow, instead climbing around to meet him on the other side. He then leads me up a chimneywide cleavage in the rock formation onto a ledge the size of our living room. Alex stands there waiting with a coterie of stuffed animals, eager to continue my tour.

The first thing Alex and Nate want to do the next morning after breakfast is further explore the big rock formation. They discover routes up, down, and around it beyond what they scouted yesterday—including a couple of exposed pitches that I'm sure would throw many parents into atrial fibrillation to see their kids on. I watch mine display the kind of nimble climbing ability and psychological comfort with what they're doing that gives me confidence they'll be okay. I want to let them experiment with their own limits and get excited about such a magnificent place.

Still, watching them scramble fairly high off the ground slices an hour off my life span. I impose another rule: no talking to each other when climbing; pay full attention to what you are doing. Penny sits at our campsite reading and drinking her life-giving java, leaving this area of child management to me. I think she would rather not see where I'm letting them go.

By midmorning, Nate and Alex plead to us, "Can we go rock climbing today?" I can't help but smile. Wherever he is, I hope Walt Disney hears them.

We drive about twenty minutes across a landscape first declared a national monument by President Franklin Roosevelt in 1936 and named a national park in 1994. Now comprising about 794,000 acres, nearly three-quarters of it wilderness, the park protects the interface between the Mojave and Colorado deserts. Its western half, above three thousand feet, lies within the Mojave, domain of the Joshua tree, *piñon* pine, juniper, scrub oak, and beavertail and prickly-pear cacti, both of which produce large, gorgeous red flowers with yellow centers. Most of the climbing routes and campgrounds are on the west side. The park's east side, below three thousand feet, falls within the Colorado Desert portion of the larger Sonoran Desert sprawling across southern Arizona and northwestern Mexico. This is the classic, baked Southwestern desert of popular imagery, dominated by the creosote bush and home to ocotillo, "jumping cholla" cactus, and western diamondback rattlesnakes. Hundreds of geologic faults crisscross Joshua Tree, including the San Andreas along the park's southern border.

Driving past Hidden Valley, once a hideout for cattle rustlers and now the campground that usually fills first, mostly with climbers, we reach Quail Springs and a parking lot beside the ingloriously named Trash Can Rock formation.

A little while later, I'm thirty feet up a cliff face, balanced on the balls of my feet, my fingers clinging to cracks. My 160 pounds rest largely on the minimal friction between a tiny area of sticky rubber on the outsoles of my climbing shoes and the granite's coarse surface. Into my head pops a question I have confronted inestimable numbers of times, whenever I haven't climbed for months: why does this seem so hard and scary?

To a nonclimber, the question might sound like a joke. But I'm on a very easy route, a fifty-foot-high slab we chose so that Nate and Alex would have a chance at getting up it. Its difficulty is rated several grades below the level at which I've climbed for years. I should be scaling it with ease; instead, I'm hesitant and nervous. It's a reminder of how rarely I climb and that this sport is one part ability and two parts head game.

Much of this sport's appeal is how it singularly focuses the mind on this immediate physical task: being high off the ground, with the prospect of falling always imminent, has a way of commanding your undivided attention. For many people, the fear would be paralyzing. But some find the means to channel that stress into positive motivation, and it's a powerful drug. Erasing all thoughts and background concerns from your mind is an incredibly rejuvenating and rare experience in modern life. I've gotten to the top of a pitch to realize that, for the twenty or forty or however many minutes I was moving, my focus had tunneled in so myopically that I'd actually forgotten where I was beyond that cliff face in front of my eyes.

Deprivation of something challenging but cherished can either make you quit it entirely or long for it even more deeply; for me, it's been the latter. Seeing climbers out here resurrects visceral memories. Watching them—most young and no doubt childless—feels like bumping into the girl you never got over, with her husband.

On the ground below me, Penny stands belaying my rope, ready to catch me if I fall. Alex sits at a nearby picnic table reading a book and occasionally lobbing distracting questions at Penny: "Where's the water?" (Right next to you.) "Can I get a snack?" (Look in the car.) Nate practices placing a few pieces of gear I've given him into cracks at the base of the cliff. I've begun teaching him how to insert the cams, nuts, and other hardware securely enough to hold his falling weight—and how to remove them, as the climber following must do. I think he's more interested in the associated hardware than the actual act of climbing. To him, this sport is like Legos for grown-ups.

I lumber gracelessly to the top and set up the rope so that everyone can give this easy route a try. Alex wants to go first. I climb beside her for moral support and a little boost when needed—but she manages it mostly without help. Only when Penny's lowering us back to flat earth does Alex shed a few, brief tears over the disconcerting sensation of having to lean back over the void and trust the rope to hold her. Nate follows, uninterested in my escort, grunting and panting like a seasoned adult climber.

At the top, wide-eyed, he confesses to me, "That was harder than I thought it would be." Amazing how often my son and I see eye to eye.

In the afternoon, driving back to our campsite across that Seussian landscape, I try to imagine it without Joshua trees. Sure, the rock formations are spectacular. But absent the trees, with only scraggly vegetation typical of lower, hotter deserts growing here, it would be like Yosemite Valley without the waterfalls or Glacier National Park without the glaciers: a critical element will have departed.

I ask Penny whether she thinks this place will look bereft without the trees.

"Absolutely. Totally," she says without hesitation. "The trees are what make this park what it is."

KEN COLE, THE U.S. Geological Survey research ecologist behind the article predicting that the Joshua tree will one day cease to exist in this park, has studied how past changes in climate have affected vegetation patterns on a landscape scale.

About 11,700 years ago, the world's climate warmed by several degrees Fahrenheit in less than a century. That ended the last ice age and marked the close of the Pleistocene Epoch and the beginning of our current Holocene Epoch. Fingerprints of the shift have been found across the Northern Hemisphere. Asian deserts received more moisture. In North America, mean temperatures rose from the Grand Canyon to the ocean's surface off the coast of Northern California. And in the region we now call the desert Southwest, the range of the Joshua tree contracted.

Fossilized findings in pack rat middens indicate that between 22,000 and 11,700 years ago, Joshua trees were the dominant flora across the Mojave and Sonoran deserts, growing several hundred feet lower in elevation than they do today. But by the time the Holocene was a few thousand years old, the tree's range had shrunk to its current margins.

The data reveal something critical to the survival prospects of *Yucca brevifolia:* the warm Holocene climate should have allowed the tree to expand northward. But it basically hasn't.

Topography erects one obstacle. Cold winters and too much snow prevent it from infiltrating higher terrain on the edges of its range, while brutally hot, arid summers keep it out of lower ground. June droughts to the west and August monsoons to the east have similar limiting effects.

But it really comes down to simple math: rodents disperse seeds no more than forty meters (about 130 feet) from the source tree. Each new Joshua tree does not produce viable seeds until it reaches about twenty years old. That represents a migration rate of two meters—little more than six feet—per year since the Holocene began.

The Joshua tree is in a race in which it cannot remotely compete. As Cole noted, and as a 2003 article in the prestigious journal *Nature* observed, climatic zones have been shifting on average six kilometers per decade, or six hundred meters per year. Crawling two meters per year leaves the Joshua woefully far off that pace.

Field observations made in recent decades support the conclusion that Joshua trees are not reproducing in the park. According to Cole's article, few trees have sprung up at the site of a wildfire forty-seven years ago, or at another spot where trees were cut to plow a field seventy years ago. While new Joshuas are sprouting farther north, in California's Inyo Mountains and Eureka Valley, the saplings typically stand within a hundred feet of a mature tree.

"I look at Joshua trees as a worst-case scenario as far as the impacts of climate change," Cole told me.

More optimistically, areas of east-central California, southern Nevada and Utah, and northwestern Arizona may become hospitable to Joshua trees in the new climate regime. The federal government owns more than 80 percent of that land, creating the potential for "assisted relocation" of the species. But that would require a controversial—and expensive—new approach to managing endangered species through direct manipulation. With estimates of 400,000 species going extinct if worldwide average temperature increases 2 degrees Celsius, or 3.6 degrees Fahrenheit—the minimum expected—it is hard to imagine we will save many of them.

While Cole does not foresee extinction "anytime soon," he told me, "I have no qualms saying the Joshua tree will not be able to reproduce in Joshua Tree National Park in seventy years." Some older trees will remain, "but it's unlikely they'll be able to produce viable seedlings."

Cameron Barrows offers a less dire outlook. Barrows is a research ecologist at the University of California–Riverside's Center for Conservation Biology. Months after our visit here, in a March 2011 report, he predicted that 31 percent of current Joshua tree habitat in the park would still support healthy, reproducing trees with the 2 degrees Celsius temperature rise expected over the next fifty years. He told me that, unlike Cole's, his methodology accounted more precisely for topographical and rainfall variation across the park. So his study more readily identified microclimates where the tree could persevere.

"I am more optimistic than others," Barrows said.

Still, his data also find that the tree's suitable park habitat would all but disappear—shrinking to 1 percent of its current coverage—if temperatures spike by 3 degrees Celsius, or 5.4 degrees Fahrenheit.

"The problem with predicting is that we don't know how we are going to respond to climate change," Barrows said, alluding to the uncertain course of international efforts to reduce carbon dioxide emissions. "I'm uncomfortable predicting beyond fifty years. We're pretty sure it's going to be at least two degrees warmer, but is it going to be three, four, five degrees Celsius? We don't know."

Todd Esque, another U.S. Geological Survey research scientist, agrees that not enough is known to see into the Joshua tree's future with high confidence. He has embarked on a long-term study measuring Joshua trees at 250 sites in five parks: Joshua Tree and Death Valley national parks, Mojave National Preserve, Lake Mead National Recreation Area, and Grand Canyon-Parashant National Monument.

Although Esque told me his team has not seen any new Joshua trees emerge on any of those 250 sites since they began two years ago, he hypothesizes that "desert species may go several years without any new recruitment." He has found evidence, for instance, that blackbrush, a common desert shrub, germinates only every forty years.

And yet, he added, "I'm not terribly optimistic. We're chopping up the desert into smaller pieces with development. So as far as having healthy, open spaces of desert, we may [eliminate] that before climate change does."

The Joshua tree's plight illustrates adaptation challenges that many species will face as the climate warms: they will not survive in their native habitat, they do not migrate effectively, and besides topographical barriers, there are a lot of highways, cities, suburbs, and other manmade obstacles standing in their way.

There's another piece to the Joshua's story that no one knows the answer to: what rising temperatures will do to the yucca moth. Without it, Joshua trees could not pollinate, and all the computer models would become just so much digital tumbleweed.

Few people have examined the Joshua tree's modern reproductive success as intimately or as long as James Cornett. A desert ecologist and retired museum director and curator in Palm Springs, California, Cornett teaches a course at the UC–Riverside Palm Desert Campus called Ecology of the Joshua Tree.

For twenty years beginning in 1988, Cornett monitored the trees on three one-hectare (roughly two-and-a-half-acre) plots in Joshua Tree National Park that had "reasonably decent stands of Joshua trees on them." The sites differ greatly in elevation and rainfall. At all three, the number of trees declined "significantly," he told me—by 16 percent at Upper Covington Flat, 25 percent in Lost Horse Valley, and 60 percent in Queen Valley.

"The immediate cause for death appeared to be two severe droughts," he said. Between 1999 and 2004, the mean precipitation at nearby

Indio, California, was 1.4 inches a year, and 0.14 inch of rain fell in 2002, compared to a long-term mean of an already parched 3.3 inches per year.

Upper Covington Flat had long been the "most favorable site for Joshua trees anywhere in the park," Cornett told me. In the 1980s, seven of the ten largest known Joshua trees grew there. "If Joshua trees are struggling in the best part of the park for them, I think it's a fait accompli that they're not going to make it," he said. He has also compared photos from recent years to older pictures dating back as far as a century, which showed the decline in Joshua trees has been going on for at least three decades.

His study subjects included three "giant" Joshuas that he described as "extraordinarily healthy" in the early 1990s. One, in Queen Valley nicknamed "Emily's Tree" was the tallest known Joshua, standing almost forty-two feet with a trunk circumference of nearly nine feet. A second, a thirty-two-footer called "Giant" at Upper Covington, was the third-largest known Joshua. The third specimen grew outside the park. All died by 2002. All three, Cornett pointed out, had undoubtedly survived numerous previous droughts. This time, they didn't.

Perhaps more tellingly, among all three study sites just one new tree sprouted, in Lost Horse Valley. It died before his project ended in 2008.

"When I first heard about Ken Cole's modeling of climate change and what might happen, I was a critic of his conclusions. I generally felt that Joshua trees would survive in the higher areas of the park," Cornett told me. "I'm in perfect agreement with him now. We have field data that proves what he predicted is coming true."

After a pause, Cornett remarked, "National parks were supposed to be forever. That whole premise is vanishing before our eyes."

NATE AND I PAUSE partway up a long, fingerlike ridge of stone extending off a rock formation at least three hundred feet tall. Precipitous drop-offs a half step to either side of us await a slight slip or a trip—a scenario I prefer to not picture. I've told Nate to sit where he is and not move. Penny and Alex are sitting and snacking far below us, oblivious to our circumstances. Peering up at the narrow, blocky jumble above us, like a row of granite sofas stacked at sharp angles and climbing into the sky, I feel decidedly hesitant about scrambling farther up it with my son.

Nate insists that we go to the top.

I've disappointed him repeatedly today, our last day in the park. While we packed up our camping gear this morning, he saw several young people clamber to the very top of the kid fort—a summit I'd already forbidden to my kids because there was a chance they could take a bad fall.

We drove here, to the park's Wonderland of Rocks, a chaotic constellation of massive boulders and towering cliffs that looks like a bombed-out city built of stone. On an easy route up a sixty-foot cliff, I realized that the crack I was climbing flared too widely to accept any protective gear, so I backed down. Penny, of course, was relieved at my choice, and Alex seemed unperturbed. But Nate was crushed for a second time.

Now I'm scrutinizing this ridge, wondering whether I can get him up and down it safely. Instructing him to wait—not moving a centimeter—I scramble thirty feet ahead, scouting the moves. As sometimes happens, it's not as hard as it looked. I backtrack to him and guide him carefully up a little farther, ready to catch him if he slips. In this slow, methodical manner, we inch upward, exploring around each turn, traversing ledges, and finally crawling up through one chimneylike passage and popping out onto the tablelike top of the rock formation.

Nate beams, looking around but barely moving, intimidated by the exposure all around us. He mutters the usual "Wow!" and "This is awesome," but says very little else, his silence perhaps the best measure of his astonishment at making it up here. Though I would not have come up if I thought it was unsafe, I'm glad we did it. That feeling of disbelief, of having attained what seemed impossibly far beyond your reach, is the holy grail of climbing, and my son's awash in it right now.

We sit down. I put an arm around his small, bony shoulders, and he wraps both arms around my ribs. I talk to him about evaluating risk, weighing the possibility of a fall against the consequences—trying to make him see that when the consequences are potentially severe, you do not accept even what seems like minimal risk.

Before making the slow, careful descent of our route, Nate and I enjoy a few more quiet minutes admiring our bird's-eye view of the Wonderland of Rocks, a roiling sea of stone that, for now, remains speckled with Joshua trees.

A forest, however scraggly, does not vanish overnight. As in James Cornett's study plots, these high-desert plateaus of Joshua trees appear doomed to steadily thin out as the park grows increasingly inhospitable to *Yucca brevifolia*. Trees will die without new ones replacing them. Trunks will topple over and decay; other desert flora will spring up around them. Survivors will hang on in shrinking refuges, visited by tourists who want to see the last Joshua trees in Joshua Tree National Park.

And one day, probably during a drought, the last Joshua tree in the park will perish, like the last truffula tree chopped down in *The Lorax*.

When Nate and Alex were very young, I read that Dr. Seuss book to them so many times that, for a while, I had much of it memorized. Published in 1971—when I was Nate's age—the classic fable about industrial development, environmental exploitation, and shortsighted greed tells a fictional story about the steady destruction of a forest of brightly colored truffula trees and the host of creatures that lived there. *The Lorax* ends with the Once-ler, the character responsible for the catastrophe, handing off the last remaining truffula tree seed to a young boy, urging him to embrace a vision for the future that allows a space for the trees to flourish again.

For the magnificent Joshua tree, the lord of the desert, that place may one day no longer be the park named for it. But the Joshua might endure somewhere—and like the fictional truffula tree, stand as a symbol of both exploitation and hope.

Lower Yellowstone Falls in the Grand Canyon of the
Yellowstone River, Yellowstone National Park, Wyoming.

CHAPTER 9

THE END OF WINTER

JANUARY 2011

Snow flies horizontally on icy bursts of wind that rub our faces raw. The short, widely spaced evergreens growing alongside the cross-country ski trail are trimmed in white. Through the gauzy air flooded with powder, we can barely see the sheer walls of the Black Canyon of the Yellowstone River just a few miles away and a thousand feet below us.

Watching the snowstorm paint everything with a fresh coat of white, I'm thinking that I could ski a thousand days through snow falling on forests and mountains and each time it would feel like the world made brand-new again.

Penny sprints ahead, turns around and returns to us, then spins and sprints ahead again. She starts and stops her watch's chronograph whenever we start and stop skiing; in her mind, all physical activity is training that demands a precise accounting to the second. When we pause at a view, I hear a soft electronic beep drift over from her general direction, giving new meaning to the notion of scenery that stops time.

Alex and Nate, who first got on skis shortly after they first stood up, take off into the wind-driven snow as if those skinny boards were anatomical extensions of their skinny legs.

Looking around, I observe aloud that we have seen only a couple of other people out here amid the world's most famous limestone terraces at Mammoth Hot Springs in Yellowstone National Park.

"Maybe," Alex says without a trace of sarcasm, trying to be helpful, "it's because it's really windy and snow goes in your face."

Although not yet eight years old, my astute daughter has a knack for boiling any situation down to its salient truth. Of course, by the time a second-grader has revealed the stunningly obvious to you, it is too late to suggest that this may have already crossed your mind.

We glide over frozen ground toward billowing clouds of steam rising from the earth. At a patch of wind-scoured snow, we step out of our skis and descend wooden steps to a boardwalk snaking across the hot springs terraces. Steaming water trickles over a seemingly infinite series of shallow pools spilling hundreds of feet down this hillside. Abstract patterns in sugary white, gold, green, orange, rust, and brown color the pool bottoms vividly, a surreal contrast against the snowy ground. Downhill from us, elk loiter in the warm air by the springs.

We bend down to look at leaves and tips of pine boughs that have fallen into the pools and grown a crenellated edging of calcium crystals. Nate's eyes widen as he softly mutters, "That's so cool!" He and Alex hurry to the next pool.

But the wind slices to bone and soon we need to generate some warmth. We click back into our skis and continue around Mammoth's rolling, mile-and-a-half-long Upper Terraces Loop, past gnarled pine trees, past an odd-looking mound with white and tan mineral streaks spilling down its sides, and down a long hill through pine forest hushed by winter.

Back in our room at the Mammoth Hot Springs Hotel, we peel off damp clothes and slowly shake off the chill. Given time and abetted by wind, cold can soak into flesh like a marinade. It will surreptitiously draw heat from your body faster than metabolism's furnace produces it, until you realize your jaw will not form words properly and your hands and feet feel like cordwood.

But in reality, for Yellowstone in the middle of January, today's temperatures of a few degrees below freezing constituted a heat wave, not even approaching the deep freezes for which Yellowstone winters are legendary. Extended spells of nights plunging to minus-30 degrees Celsius and minus-40 degrees Fahrenheit, and days never rising above zero, salt the tales of many who have worked or lived in the park. The 1933 day that hit minus-66 degrees Fahrenheit was the third-coldest ever recorded in the contiguous United States. In fact, of the fifteen coldest temperatures on record in the Lower 48, six occurred in the Greater Yellowstone region.

We have come to the world's first national park ostensibly to ski tour for four days to some of Yellowstone's signature landmarks. We want to see big animals you cannot see in most of the country, to admire the delicate architecture of frozen waterfalls, and immerse ourselves in one of the most distinctive and best-preserved original landscapes on the planet.

And we have come in winter because Yellowstone looks her best in white. Her endlessly rolling lodgepole pine forests are brighter and tidier under several feet of snow. Elk, bison, and other animals migrate to the valleys in winter, and the wolves, coyotes, eagles, and other predators follow them. There is no better place and season for sighting the megafauna that populated North America before we crowded them out. For those of a certain mindset, there is only one way to explore Yellowstone: on cross-country skis or snowshoes, packing extra warm clothes and a tolerance for cold.

You can see, hear, and feel a land still wild, imagine the continent young again. In winter, Yellowstone shows her soul. But winter, sadly, is shrinking.

I STOPPED IN MY ski tracks and leaned forward, struggling to discern the snow-covered ground ahead of me in the milky blizzard. It was a freezing morning in February 2000. Near the end of a three-day trip in Yellowstone's Lamar Valley, I skied into the mounting squall, hoping to find my way back to my car before the storm peaked.

I could barely see my outstretched, gloved hand through the wind-driven snow. The whiteout left me completely disoriented, jamming my brain's sense of direction. I imagined this was the closest that a sighted person could come to understanding blindness.

Nonetheless, I had stopped because something seemed not right just ahead. Probing for some point to focus on, my eyes gradually found my ski tips projecting over the edge of a high snowbank. Beyond it, a vague, swimming grayness resolved into a rocky creek several feet below me. I had nearly plunged into it.

My wife of less than two years was home, pregnant with our son. I was alone.

Two winters later, two friends and I embarked on a seven-day traverse of Yellowstone's Bechler Canyon region. We skied all day and slept through nights below zero Fahrenheit. Then it snowed—harder than I've ever seen, more than five feet of fresh powder over two days. At the storm's height, we wallowed thigh-deep in feathery snow and covered barely more than a mile in eight exhausting hours.

When I returned in early March 2005 to write a magazine story, I cross-country skied in shirtsleeves, under a sun that made it feel like June. And just a year ago, in January 2010, Penny and I ski toured with the kids across the park's Upper Geyser Basin wearing only light fleece jackets.

Of course, personal anecdotes are not scientific data. But they illustrate what has been documented.

Data from a U.S. Historical Climatology network weather station at Mammoth show that the average temperature of the past two decades was 1.7 degrees Fahrenheit warmer than the twentieth-century average. A March 2011 article in the *Journal of Climate,* published by the American Meteorological Society, concluded that snow across the Northern Rockies—including Yellowstone—melted out an average of eight days earlier in 2007 than in 1969, and covered the ground for two fewer weeks during the year. Since 1985, the growing season in the park—the number of days the temperature rises above freezing—has increased by a staggering twenty-five days. The seven earliest dates on record for Yellowstone Lake's ice-out have occurred in the past thirty years.

Tom Olliff has seen how winters have warmed. Now the National Park Service coordinator of the Great Northern Landscape Conservation Cooperative, or GNLCC, working on conservation from southern Wyoming to the Canadian Rockies, he first came to Yellowstone as a college student in the summer of 1977 to pump gas at Fishing Bridge. He has since held almost every job in the park, from backcountry ranger to firefighter, from search and rescue to director of resources.

When he lived in Canyon, Old Faithful and Grant Village in the mid-1980s and early 1990s, he told me, "It was routine to have a two-week period when the temperature never got above twenty below [zero]. Recently, we just haven't had these really deep cold spells like you had back in those days."

More than any other park outside Alaska, Yellowstone preserves a slice of the West as it appeared two centuries ago to the Lewis and Clark expedition (which passed just north of the area, missing it entirely). That is largely because Yellowstone National Park was established so early, in 1872, just a few years after the first organized efforts to explore it. That was near the height of the slaughter of the great bison herds, and two years before a rancher told Theodore Roosevelt that he had traveled a thousand miles across the West and was "never out of sight of a dead buffalo, and never in sight of a live one."

Just two hundred bison remained in Yellowstone by 1874; today, an estimated three thousand roam the park's grasslands. The number of grizzly bears in the park has quadrupled to more than six hundred since the bear was listed as threatened, in 1975, according to the Interagency Grizzly Bear Committee. The last resident gray wolf in Yellowstone was killed in 1926, but in 1995 and 1996, thirty-one wolves from Canada were reintroduced in the Lamar Valley. Their population has since expanded to more than three hundred.

Over 90 percent of Yellowstone's more than three million annual visitors come during summer. Most will join a crowd of five hundred tourists watching Old Faithful erupt, get stuck in traffic jams in the Hayden Valley, and walk five minutes from their vehicles to overlooks at Mammoth Hot Springs and the Grand Canyon of the Yellowstone River.

When I think about Yellowstone, I picture rolling plains of clean snow. I recall standing on a windblown knoll on a February day so frigid I had an ice-cream headache, watching a wolf pack pour like an avalanche off a nearby hillside onto a herd of grazing elk. As though guided by one brain, the herd leaped into flight, moving in a way both evasively chaotic and synchronized, like a white-water river.

On another morning a decade ago, I skied up a gentle valley, embraced by the absolute silence that subdues a place when deep snow covers the ground; there is no birdsong or rustling of leaves, and any animals not hibernating practice stealth either to find a meal or avoid becoming one. A solitary wolf emerged atop a ridge devoid of vegetation and standing out in flawless white against a blue sky. Then that wolf's mates trotted into view, one by one, and launched into a hair-raising group howl.

Yellowstone is America's most popular national park for winter recreation. A quarter of a million people visit between December and March to cross-country ski, snowshoe, sightsee from a snowmobile or a snowcoach, and watch wildlife. They come to see Earth's most diverse and intact assemblage of geysers, mudpots, hot springs, and fumaroles. Travel on foot along the Firehole River or through another thermal area during the lonely quietude of winter, when steam clouds obscure the sun and evoke a land on fire, and you will glean a sense of the skin-tingling awe that nineteenth-century trapper Jim Bridger felt when he described this high plateau as "the place where Hell bubbled up."

In the world made new through rising temperatures, hell no longer merely bubbles up from the netherworld. For many living things, from trout to whitebark pine trees to grizzly bears, it's getting uncomfortably warm above ground, too.

"WE'RE REALLY LEARNING THAT climate change merely amplifies other changes that already exist," Tom Olliff of the GNLCC told me.

Since the mid-1990s, when some unknown fisherman introduced lake trout to octopus-shape Yellowstone Lake—the largest freshwater lake above seven thousand feet in North America—that nonnative fish has been gobbling up Yellowstone cutthroat trout. Cutthroat numbers measured in one major tributary creek plummeted from more than thirty thousand to around five hundred in a decade. Now, rising stream temperatures further imperil cutthroat—a key food for many animals, including coyotes, otters, and bears. Water above 73 degrees Fahrenheit kills trout. In July 2007, park officials discovered hundreds of dead trout in the Firehole River. Its waters had hit 82 degrees.

Other animals face similar threats. Wolverines, estimated at fewer than five hundred in the Lower 48, den in snow at least eight feet deep;

no one knows what less snow will mean for them. Yellowstone's long-necked, white trumpeter swans shelter themselves on lakes from coyotes and other predators. As kettle ponds have shrunk—one, Trumpeter Lake, from twenty-four acres in 1984 to about four acres today, Olliff told me—so has the swan population.

But the species of perhaps greatest concern is a tree that lives at higher elevations than any other in Greater Yellowstone.

Whitebark pine is considered both a "foundation species," meaning it creates conditions that allow other species to thrive, and a "keystone species" because of its positive impacts on biodiversity. Birds and squirrels nest in whitebark. The trees' shade delays snowmelt, preserving stream flows later into summer. And whitebark produces a seed the size of a corn kernel that, with a fat content of 52 percent, is a delicacy among more than a hundred types of winged and four-legged diners.

From August to October, Clark's nutcrackers harvest the seeds—also known as pine nuts—carrying as many as a hundred in their throat pouch and flying up to eight miles from a source tree to bury them in the ground. Each nutcracker creates thousands of caches and uses its highly developed spatial memory to later find about 70 percent of them. Red squirrels also cache pine nuts.

Unclaimed seed caches may germinate and grow a tree—or go straight to the top of the food chain. In late summer and autumn, bears enter a state called hyperphagia, eating almost constantly to fatten up for hibernation. They sniff out and gorge on seed caches. In years of abundant pine nuts, bears have been known to eat nothing else—even after emerging from hibernation, when they may smell seed caches beneath six feet of snow.

Studies have warned that between blister rust, beetles, and increasingly destructive wildfires, whitebark pine might not make it—with implications for many animals, including Clark's nutcrackers and that icon of wilderness, the grizzly bear. The U.S. Fish and Wildlife Service announced in July 2010 that it would review whether to place whitebark pine on the Endangered Species List.

In January 2011, the environmental organization Natural Resources Defense Council and the U.S. Forest Service reported that more than half of the two million acres of whitebark pine trees in Greater Yellowstone were dead, killed by mountain pine beetles or blister rust. Ominously, the report predicted that whitebark will be "functionally extinct" in the Yellowstone ecosystem within five to seven years.

In an article published online in the Proceedings of the National Academy of Sciences in July 2011, University of California–Merced environmental engineering professor Anthony Westerling forecasted that large wildfires will transform the Greater Yellowstone Ecosystem by midcentury; blazes comparable to the historic fires of 1988 will become almost annual events.

Olliff sees two arguments against whitebark extinction: the beetle epidemic has tapered off, and young whitebark are regenerating. Plus, he pointed out, predators—and beetles are one—do not eliminate their primary food source. Yet, Olliff acknowledged that a hotter climate does not bode well for whitebark pine. "Will this natural-disturbance regime be out of whack, with the beetle decimating the whitebark pine?" he asked. "That's the million-dollar question."

Experts disagree on how severe a blow the decline or loss of whitebark will deal to grizzlies. Bears are omnivores; they turn to carrion of winter-killed elk in spring, glacier lilies in early summer, huckleberries and army cutworm moths in late summer. Chuck Schwartz, leader of the Interagency Grizzly Study Team, and Chris Servheen, grizzly bear recovery coordinator for the U.S. Fish and Wildlife Service, among others, believe that bears would thrive even without pine nuts. They point to data showing that grizzly reproductive rates are negligibly affected by cyclical whitebark seed "bust" years.

"I don't know that I find data from several isolated bad cone years reassuring," Sierra Club western regional director Steve Thomas told *Sierra Magazine* in January 2011. "Let's see what ten consecutive bad cone years look like before we make any assumptions, because they're coming."

But most agree: in years of few pine nuts, grizzly bears come into contact with people more frequently. They come to lower elevations in search of food, get into human garbage and facilities, and attack livestock—often with deadly consequences for the bear.

Grizzlies can live twenty-five years or longer in the wild and reproduce very slowly, so population signals from shifts in food availability
are almost impossible to discern. But here is a stark fact about bear
longevity: most Greater Yellowstone grizzlies die at the hands of people.
They get hit by vehicles, mistakenly shot by hunters, and destroyed for
acts of aggression, among numerous human-instigated vectors of death.
In 2010, seventy-five grizzlies—one in eight—were killed or removed from Yellowstone. The single-year record of seventy-nine was set
just two years earlier. The annual average in this century's first decade
was nineteen.

More bear-human contact from a long-term crash in pine nuts will
undoubtedly be bad for individual bears. Will it prove catastrophic for
the entire population? We may not know for years.

THE HERD OF BISON hunkers in a swale just a few steps off Yellowstone's Grand Loop Road on the rolling, almost treeless Blacktail Deer
Plateau, east of Mammoth. I count at least thirty of the shaggy beasts.
They bury their faces in the snow, wagging their horned watermelon
heads side to side, digging down to find grass.

On our second morning in the park, we have pulled the car over
at the sight of this herd. Nate and Alex step through two feet of snow
over to a rise, where several people mill around, enjoying a close look at
North America's largest land mammal. While Penny chats with fellow
citizens of Red Sox Nation on vacation from Boston, I keep one eye on
the animals and one on our kids, keeping them at a safe distance.

Bison appear entirely docile about 98 percent of the time. The other
2 percent of the time, they have been known to flip people into the air
like pancakes.

Skiing alone across the Midway Geyser Basin several years ago, I
crested a low hillock to a sight that made my head buzz: hundreds of
bison sprawled across the broad valley as if an encampment of an occu-
pying army. In that moment of expansive solitude granted by winter, I
came as close as we moderns can get to stumbling upon one of America's
aboriginal buffalo herds, tens of thousands of animals peppering a plain
for miles.

As my eyes panned that valleywide roadblock, one animal broke into a sprint directly toward me. Seeing a bison gallop thirty miles an hour—as they can—is like seeing a grand piano suddenly sprout horns and charge you with the speed of a horse. My heart rattled somewhere between my ears. I glanced toward the one tree nearby, wondering how quickly I could get out of my skis and up it. But the rogue bison inexplicably made a ninety-degree turn and, without breaking stride, ran away from me.

Snapping back to the present, I let Alex and Nate imagine themselves stepping back two centuries to set eyes on the beast that made the continent's interior fertile. Minutes farther up the road, we stop again where several people are peering through spotting scopes—and my kids enjoy their first magnified peek at three wolves guarding a kill.

By afternoon, we are skiing up the unplowed Tower-Canyon Road. Hundreds of feet below us, the Yellowstone River knifes between orderly cliffs of columnar basalt. Sun spilling between shifting clouds dapples the river canyon with the light of Renaissance paintings. A little later, we watch Tower Fall pour 132 feet into a gorge, its ghostly motion visible through a gossamer curtain of ice encasing it. "It's amazing that it's frozen," Nate says. "I mean, it's a waterfall!"

The shattered debris at the waterfall's base indicates that pieces of this frozen chandelier have detached and crashed earthward. Although the air feels cool, I've noticed occasional droplets of water drip from branches.

In the not-very-distant past, reporting Tower Fall unfrozen in January might have sounded like a tall tale. But if several mild days like today and yesterday had preceded our visit, we may not have seen this magnificent natural ice sculpture at all.

"WHAT IF IT HAPPENED today? What if the entire park just all of a sudden blew up?!" Nate says excitedly.

My son is preoccupied with the volcanic history of Yellowstone as we ski together down another trail on the morning of our last full day in the park. His brain is churning out gallons of serotonin over the thought that we are standing atop North America's largest supervolcano *and it is active.* Like virtually any boy his age with a pulse, Nate foams at the mouth over talk of violent, mass destruction. Watching my son, it astounds me that we allow anyone who began life as a boy to command an army.

Several times over the past 2 million years, tremendous eruptions turned the earth here inside out. They left behind a caldera that spans thirty-four miles by forty-five miles, encompassing most of the park. This boiling subterranean cauldron fuels ten thousand geothermal features—half of Earth's total—including more than three hundred geysers, two-thirds of the planet's total. Scientists say the Yellowstone supervolcano, which last blew 640,000 years ago, is overdue for another eruption on a scale that could destabilize human civilization worldwide.

On some level, Nate comprehends the slim odds of the first supervolcano eruption in 640,000 years occurring, say, before lunch. Nonetheless, he clings to a shred of hope.

Our family has actually been unknowing spectators to a rare, if unspectacular, demonstration of the power simmering underground here. The region's volcanic and tectonic instability generates between a thousand and two thousand unnoticeable yet measurable earthquakes a year—usually of magnitude three or weaker. Occasional "earthquake swarms" of minor temblors occur. Over two weeks beginning January 17, 2010, 1,620 quakes rattled the park, the second-largest swarm ever recorded in the Yellowstone Caldera. We skied across the Upper Geyser Basin one day near the end of that string. Fortunately or unfortunately, depending on your perspective, we didn't feel a thing—though we did see several geysers erupt.

Nate and I have been skiing side by side while talking. But now our conversation and forward motion stop—not for anything said, but rather, for the distractingly abrupt termination of level ground.

We have emerged from the almost flat terrain and intimate sight lines of a lodgepole pine forest and halted at the brink of a chasm a thousand feet deep and a half mile across—a visual transition so jarring it seems to require a wordless pause to recalibrate our senses.

Snow blotchily paints crumbling, yellow walls of iron-tinged rhyolite, the inspiration for the park's name. Furry patches of lodgepole pine forest cling to steep slopes and isolated trees speckle the canyon, sprouting improbably from ledges too small and distant to see. The sound of the river flogging boulders far below us reaches our ears, distorted into rubbery waves by the wind and cliffs. The hypnotic maw draws your gaze into it, figuratively dragging you by the arm on a flight of the imagination, swooping downward over jagged promontories and knife-edge buttresses to V-shape whitewater rapids that look no larger than a thumbnail from up here.

I have stood before at the rim of the Grand Canyon of the Yellowstone River, in both summer and winter. I knew what to expect. But for Nate, the experience is as fresh as it was for explorer Charles W. Cook (and no doubt for countless Native Americans who happened upon it for centuries before Cook). Cook, leader of an 1869 expedition to explore the Yellowstone area, wrote in his journal about his first view of the Grand Canyon of the Yellowstone River:

> I was riding ahead, the two pack animals following, and then Mr. Folsom and Mr. Peterson on their saddle horses. I remembered seeing what appeared to be an opening in the forest ahead, which I presumed to be a park, or open country. While my attention was attracted by the pack animals, which had stopped to eat grass, my saddle horse suddenly stopped. I turned and looked forward from the brink of the great canyon, at a point just across from what is now called Inspiration Point. I sat there in amazement, while my companions came up, and after that, it seemed to me that it was five minutes before anyone spoke.

Nate looks it over, saying nothing. Maybe, like Cook and his companions, he cannot find the words to put such scenery into the proper context. Or maybe he's picturing the excellent fireworks show this yellow rock will yield in that hour of Armageddon when the supervolcano belches again.

A couple of minutes behind us, Penny and Alex glide over. We are skiing along the west rim of the Grand Canyon of the Yellowstone River, part of an all-day snowcoach tour from the Mammoth Hot Springs Hotel to Canyon. For four and a half of arguably the most breathtaking miles I have ever covered on skis, we appear to be the only people out here.

At the trail's other end, we reach Lookout Point, overlooking the thunderous column of water marking the beginning of the canyon, 308-foot-tall Lower Yellowstone Falls. The highest-volume waterfall in the Rocky Mountains pours over a cliff with a cacophony like fighter jets shredding the air. A curtain of ice the size of a city building hangs from the lip of the falls to more than halfway down the face. At the base of the waterfall, an ice mountain, built up by chunks breaking off the cliffs and the perpetual mist freezing on contact, stands more than a hundred feet tall.

The kids were showing signs of weariness and hunger before we reached Lookout Point. But now, rejuvenated by one of the original forms of entertainment—water falling and freezing—they gush over the tremendous mound of ice, the noise of the falls, our precipitous overlook at the canyon's rim.

Millions of tourists have stood here before us. Famous painters and photographers have captured this scene, beginning with Thomas Moran and William Henry Jackson in 1871.

And right now, my kids know exactly how Moran and Jackson felt.

TOM OLLIFF RECALLS THAT during his first couple of winters in Yellowstone, "I actually never left. I was a kid from Alabama who'd never seen winter and didn't want to miss a day of it. Winter, to me, is the time when you have this invisibility cloak. Laying down a blanket of snow covers up some of the scars on the landscape."

But winter has begun a slow fade. From the Alps to the U.S. Pacific Northwest and Northeast, numerous ski resorts could shut down by the time Nate and Alex are my age. One study foresees snowpack declining by half in Colorado's ski capital of Summit County and by 61 percent at Idaho's glitzy Sun Valley. In November 2010, a report from the University of California–Davis and the U.S. Geological Survey predicted that snowfall will diminish by 45 percent at the popular resorts around Lake Tahoe by midcentury.

Several weeks before this Yellowstone trip, our ski season at home in Boise began on Thanksgiving Day, when our local resort opened thanks to abundant early snow from a La Niña cycle. But the ski area last opened that early in the season in 1994. Its base sits at barely more than six thousand feet, the elevation of the rain-snow line in many winter storms now. I wonder how many years of skiing remain there.

In any season, of course, Yellowstone is special for its diversity of wildlife. Trying to peer into the future, Olliff sees that also changing.

"Fifty years out, there's potential for large shifts in vegetation and species," he told me. "For me, the effects of climate change are going to be more subtle in Yellowstone than other places. If you're an angler, you can fish the same creeks and you're going to see them change over time. If you're a hiker, you're going to see changes in the alpine areas, whitebark pine reduced. If you're a birder, you'll see some species shift—some that occur in Yellowstone now, won't [in the future], some that don't now, will."

The IPCC predicted in 2007 that 20 to 30 percent of species worldwide are at risk of extinction if average temperatures rise by between 2.7 degrees Fahrenheit (1.5 Celsius) and 4.5 degrees Fahrenheit (2.5 Celsius). Many scientists now say that a minimum 5.4 degrees Fahrenheit (3 Celsius) rise is likely in this century—which could erase 40 percent of all species. Many believe we are in the midst of the sixth mass extinction of life on Earth—and the first instigated by a single species. An October 2010 article in the journal *Science* predicted that one in five vertebrates may go away forever, thanks in part to habitat destruction, overexploitation, and invasive competitors. Climate change shoves many of these creatures over the threshold.

WHEN OUR SNOWCOACH STOPS along Norris-Canyon Road, Alex wakens from her nap lying against my side. Snow falls steadily outside. It's early afternoon; we left Canyon a half hour ago. Penny and I broach the idea of skiing one more time today, two and a half miles down the relatively flat Virginia Cascades Trail.

Nate releases a groan like the sound of an old log being rolled over after years of lying on the same patch of ground. He hasn't napped but looks as if he was knocking at sleep's door, waiting to be invited in. Alex blinks, briefly volleying this proposal back and forth in her mind, and then says, "I probably have enough energy to do it."

Nate can't very well back out now. Once we set off on our skis into the lodgepole forest, though, they both grin and chatter as if neither had even considered not going.

Plump snowflakes parachute out of a sky so blank the flakes appear to materialize five feet above us, floating there as if the air had grown dense enough to make them buoyant, as if time had downshifted. There is no wind. New snow covers up the tracks of previous skiers and the drunken stitching of shallow prints from small animals, a flawlessly clean white comforter.

The trail parallels the creek's graceful meanderings between scalloped snowbanks that overhang the black, nearly still water. The boughs of lodgepole trees, the name derived from its use in ceremonial lodges built by Native Americans, sag under the weight of thick white shawls. The forest seems to slumber contentedly, embalmed in the suffocating quiet of a windless snowstorm. It seems the acoustics could muffle a supervolcano eruption.

I think, This truly is the world made new again. At my age, that feels like an astonishing gift.

Nate and Alex certainly see their world as if it has recently sprung from nothingness for their sole enjoyment. They dwell in this momentary magic kingdom of childhood, old and intelligent enough to basically comprehend how their universe came to be, yet young and fortunately naïve enough to delight in their discovery of its intricacies, as if they are the first to see crystalline patterns in Mammoth Hot Springs, or the translucent curtain of ice over Tower Fall, or the mountain of ice below Lower Yellowstone Falls.

So Penny and I get to see these small, beautiful events for the first time again—not because these sensations have slipped between the fingers of memory, but because our children remind us that there are few joys more powerful than discovery. They transport us back there.

Trailing behind, Alex and I start loudly singing the three Christmas songs she knows well: "Rudolph, the Red-Nosed Reindeer," "Up on the Housetop," and "Jingle Bells." As snowflakes accumulate like talcum powder on our hats and shoulders, we sing those tunes over and over, partly because nothing gets old when you're seven—and partly, I believe, because we are caught in a spell that derives its power from a season called winter.

Great egret, Everglades National Park, Florida.

CHAPTER 10

GOING UNDER

Whoever said there are no straight lines in nature had never been to South Florida.

One's first impression of the Everglades is of overwhelming, almost oppressive flatness. In every direction, the eye traces a planar landscape that would hardly wobble the air bubble in a carpenter's level. There is not a moraine, drumlin, or low rise like you have seen in places that once bore the weight of ice age glaciers. There are no distant foothills, piedmonts, or uplifts causing the horizon to deviate from its Euclidian geometry.

Even the forest reinforces the perception of a globe deflated, a pancaked planet. The trees grow just twenty or thirty feet tall, and brush fills in the understory to the density of a jungle, creating a visually impenetrable wall of flora. Against the extremely horizontal topography, this uniform strip of forest between sky and water has the appearance of a highway center line painted in green.

The second thing you notice about the Everglades is the preponderance of water. It is everywhere, in sloughs, ponds, and canals, immotile and murky. It pools at the feet of tall grasses, mangroves, and cypress trees where there should be soil. The 'Glades suggest a cellar chronically inundated with standing water.

First impressions sometimes mislead. In the case of the Everglades, though, these two immediately manifest physical characteristics—the tyranny of flatness and insidious presence of water—explain almost everything about this continental appendage. They coauthored its history and will dictate its future.

UNDER A HOT SUN and cloudless sky, we shove off from a postage-stamp spot of sandy beach into the seemingly unmoving, toffee-smooth East River, just outside the northwest boundary of Everglades National Park. Nate and I share one two-person kayak, Alex and Penny another. We are setting out for a few hours of paddling this river's pondlike open stretches and tight mangrove tunnels, all protected within the Fakahatchee Strand State Preserve. A park billed as "the Amazon of North America," the Fakahatchee Strand harbors within its hundred square miles forty-four kinds of native orchids, Florida panthers, and the only forests on Earth where bald cypress and royal palm trees cohabitate.

We are here instead of kayaking the famous mangrove tunnels of the Turner River, just a few miles away in Everglades National Park, at the strong recommendation of our companion today, Justin Shurr. Justin and his wife, Alli, run Shurr Adventure Company, guiding trips in the Everglades. When he and I spoke on the phone last night, shortly after Penny, the kids, and I landed at Miami International Airport, he related a story that made a persuasive case for choosing the East over the Turner.

Just two days ago, Justin was paddling the Turner's claustrophobic mangrove tunnels, where you constantly pass within five or six feet of alligators longer than a kayak. Without warning, a twelve-foot-long gator torpedoed toward him. As he paddled backward, the gator kept coming, backing him up twenty feet before abandoning its pursuit. There are an awful darn lot of alligators in the 'Glades. But in nine years of frequent trips here, that had never happened to him. Maybe they are just coming out of their winter torpor; maybe the crowds of paddlers are irritating them. Whatever the reason, Justin told me, "the gators are getting aggressive on the Turner."

When I repeated this to Penny last night, the blood drained from her face. After regaining her voice, she responded, "You're telling me this *now?*"—as in, *before* we kayak the river? My wife has a powerful fear of alligators, and oddly enough, my pointing out the infrequency of gator attacks on people has failed to put her at ease. I smiled at her, which I do when it seems necessary to remind her that I'm trustworthy, and said, "I'm sharing this information on a need-to-know basis." She forced an insincere chuckle at this intended joke—not "ha-ha that's funny" so much as "ha-ha, this stops being funny the instant an alligator swims toward my kayak."

Minutes after launching, we get an introduction to the rich life here beyond the proliferation of mega-reptiles.

Flocks of seven or eight snowy egrets fly in close formation over our kayaks. White ibises and black anhingas flap above the wide, dark-chocolate river and the green walls flanking it. Great blue herons lift off as if from the deck of a carrier, glide on wings whose span equals my height, and set down at the water's edge to stand like feathered statuary, their stillness rendering them almost invisible.

Ungainly brown pelicans become an instant favorite of ours; this bird could be an inspiration to every awkward adolescent. With its odd, elongated beak, the pelican looks too top-heavy to ever liberate itself from the two-dimensional earth, and about as aerodynamic as a block of wood. In flight, though, it embodies grace, soaring effortlessly just above the water's surface.

But I like watching them land. They slam heavily onto the branches of spindly trees, bending them over violently before the overwhelmed tree whips back upright, the pelican bobbing dumbly until the tree regains a stooped equilibrium. Or, wings flapping in wild panic, they crash into the river in a way that evokes the full meaning of the phrase "water landing" when spoken by a flight attendant—as if this is an unpracticed, unexpected event that may not end well.

Justin points ahead at a small piece of floating driftwood, an easily overlooked shadow amid the sparkling of sunshine off the black-tea water. But it is not a piece of driftwood.

"That's a gator," he says. Only the alligator's head barely breaks the surface; its long dinosaur body and thick tail float out of sight beneath the liquid mirror. But, Justin explains, you can estimate its size using a simple, reliable formula: every inch of distance from its eyes to the end of its snout translates to a foot of body length. "That's a twelve-footer," he says.

We paddle a wide arc around the driftwood.

Justin points out several more gators, all of them at a comforting distance, each time calling out its length: "That's an eleven-footer. Those are ten- or eleven-footers."

With the river so shallow that we can often touch its bottom with our paddles, we occasionally notice gators lurking, motionless, a foot or two below the surface. The sight of them prompts me to contemplate the thin hulls of our plastic boats, which strike me as offering as much protection as oversized tub toys.

When I first found Justin's company on the Web months ago, he had assured me that we had little to fear from alligators. He wrote in one e-mail: "In winter, gators are so inactive you could sit on one." Back at home, this had become a joke with Alex and Nate after I promised to do just that. Now they remind me of my pledge.

"Hey, Dad, when are you going to sit on an alligator?" Nate prods me. "Yeaaa, when?" Alex says, giggling conspiratorially.

"As soon as we find one that's big enough," I tell them. "I don't want to squash one of these little guys."

We paddle into the first of a series of five mangrove tunnels—snaking avenues hundreds of feet long and not much wider than the kayaks. Dense tangles of trunks and limbs spring from the swampy water on each side, standing atop birdcagelike root domes. Branches arch within reach overhead, weaving together intricately, a ceiling of vipers. At times we simply grab branches to pull ourselves forward, or employ our paddles as poles, pushing off the river bottom. Nate marvels at the cumulous swirls of dark muck we stir up.

From behind me, Penny screams. I spin around in time to see her duck as something large jets past her head. An anhinga—a bird almost three feet long, with a neck like a snake—had just exploded from a hidden spot in the mangroves. "A flyby!" Justin says. "That's a rare treat!"

The kids grow quiet, frisking our surroundings with wide eyes. First we enter a Jurassic environment of alligators and giant birds, now this arboreal funhouse—the oddities just in our first morning in the Everglades have them brimming with expectation, on the verge of bursting. When our kayaks gently bump each other in a tunnel and Alex and I find ourselves suddenly face to face, a laugh boiling up from some deep shaft of joy and fascination erupts from her.

In an open stretch a few miles downriver, we turn around to retrace our route. With no perceptible current, paddling will pose no more challenge upstream than downstream.

I look out over water, mangroves, and grasslands, an insistently flat, waterlogged expanse that is not river nor lake nor land but some incomprehensible mishmash of all three, and see the story of Everglades National Park expressed in simple geographic terms. For while the future in a new climate regime remains flush with uncertainties, it holds out this immutable certainty: the ocean will rise higher and higher for a very long time to come.

SPEAKING STRICTLY IN A maritime context, South Florida is barely above water.

A six-foot man standing on an Everglades beach stretching his arms overhead would reach higher than any point of land in a million and a half acres of national park. But if he stood in the same spot at different times in prehistory, he would variously stand high and dry or deep below the ocean.

With the ebb and flow of ice ages, the ocean has alternately invaded and retreated from the region across time spans that reduce human civilization to the equivalent of an infant's first two days. During interglacial periods, like one that occurred about 125,000 years ago, sea level was as much as twenty-five feet higher than today. For having lain below sea level for much of its prehistory, South Florida rests atop a foundation of limestone up to a hundred feet thick, the sediment of millions of years of accumulated dead marine creatures.

The last ice age dropped seas far below today's level. But as glaciers started retreating 19,000 years ago, the oceans rose about four hundred feet (more than 120 meters) over roughly 13,000 years, averaging a bit more than three feet per century. The area of the present-day Everglades eventually became a freshwater basin, where dead plants and critters accumulated underwater atop the limestone bedrock. Without oxygen to facilitate the aerobic decomposition of this stuff, peat—or, in lay terminology, "muck"—piled up to eighteen feet thick.

Once sea level stabilized about 3,200 years ago, coastal and freshwater wetlands expanded. North America's largest mangrove ecosystem lined the coast, growing upon and contributing to the peat that formed low, natural levees preventing the sea from overtaking the continent's biggest freshwater saw-grass prairie, which spread over two and a half million acres.

Slide your fingers under the edge of a table and lift it ever so slightly off the floor, and it will exceed the tilt of Florida south of Lake Okeechobee, the headwaters of the Everglades. The land here—and "land" is employed loosely—rises just three inches per mile from Florida Bay inland. Known to locals as "The Lake" or "The Big O," the seventh-largest freshwater lake in the United States covers 730 square miles and holds a trillion gallons of water, yet averages only nine feet deep. Its waters spill over a natural peat dam at the lake's southern edge, discharging a current that defies any conventional notion of a river.

A "laminar flow" up to fifty miles wide and just one to three feet deep creeps south a hundred feet per day—marginally faster than some glaciers. This flow differentiates into various sloughs (pronounced "slews"), marshy, shallow, natural channels that carry the water across Everglades National Park. The famous river of grass supports pinelands, hardwood hammocks, cypress stands, saw grass, mangroves, and a tremendous variety of wildlife before draining into Florida Bay and the Gulf of Mexico.

The area's native tribes called it *Pa-hay-okee*, or "grassy water." Spanish mapmakers labeled that unknown blank space *El Laguno del Espiritu Santo*, or "the lagoon of the saints' spirits." An 1823 map of Florida was the first to call the area the Everglades.

We can only imagine the great flocks of birds that once darkened the daytime skies over the 'Glades. John James Audubon wrote about a visit to South Florida in the early 1830s: "We observed great flocks of wading birds flying overhead toward their evening roosts . . . They appeared in such numbers to actually block out the light from the sun for some time."

Developers dug the first canals in the 1880s, chasing the dream of reclaiming the vast, dismal swamp for agriculture and development. The hunting of wading birds to sell their colorful plumes for ladies' hats decimated populations, which are down 93 percent since the early twentieth century. That slaughter catalyzed the movement to protect the area.

In 1947, President Harry Truman dedicated 460,000 acres as Everglades National Park. It has since been expanded to a million and a half acres, the third-largest national park in the contiguous United States—bigger than Glacier or Grand Canyon, twice the size of Yosemite. Recognized as one of Earth's greatest wildlife sanctuaries, Everglades is home to sixteen types of wading birds, and more than 350 species of birds have been sighted here. There are almost three hundred kinds of fish. The diversity includes thirty-six vertebrates and twenty-six plant species listed as endangered, threatened, or under consideration for listing. The park is a Wetland of International Importance under the Ramsar Convention of 1987, a UNESCO International Biosphere Reserve, and a World Heritage Site.

A year after the park's creation, Congress authorized a massive project to build canals, levees, and roads crisscrossing South Florida— draining half of the original wetlands for agriculture and cities and sucking up The Big O's water before it reaches the park.

That water-diversion system is now choking off the ecosystem's ability to repel an advancing ocean.

No major U.S. national park is more vulnerable to sea-level rise than Everglades. Most of the park would be inundated by an ocean rise of two feet—which the 2007 report of the IPCC forecasted is possible by the end of this century, depending on future CO_2 emissions. But many researchers now project the ocean rising by three to six feet. The wild cards are the unpredictable melting rates of the ice caps covering West Antarctica and Greenland, oceans of frozen freshwater that are undergoing dynamic changes. They hold enough water to raise global sea level by sixteen feet and twenty-three feet, respectively. Satellite images show the West Antarctic ice is thinning and could collapse, while the geologic record reveals that much of Greenland was once ice-free—at a time when sea level was high enough to inundate the homes of half of today's global population.

Little wonder that Orrin Pilkey, described in a 2010 *New York Times* story as "one of the deans of American coastal studies," advises communities to plan for a rise of at least five feet by 2100. That same story quoted Australian sea-level expert John A. Church saying, "We can't afford to protect everything. We will have to abandon some areas."

Meanwhile, the ocean steadily creeps up on this big, shallow swamp in South Florida.

AT HIGH TIDE, THE Ten Thousand Islands in Everglades National Park perpetrate a grand illusion, giving the impression of an archipelago bobbing upon deep waters. But in reality, the island chain sits in water often shallow enough to stand up in. It is like a very large pan that fills when the tide rolls in and nearly empties when the sea retreats.

Launching our two canoes into Chokoloskee Bay at 7:30 a.m. on our second windless, sunny morning in the Everglades, we set out across a plain of saltwater showing not even a ripple. We roused the kids before dawn in order to depart on the outgoing tide, not only to use its momentum to help propel us out to the islands, but also because much of this expansive bay will transform to mudflats by early afternoon, when the tide is low.

As we will be reminded of repeatedly over the next three days of canoeing and camping out here, boating in the Ten Thousand Islands is all about timing.

We cross the broad bay to islands of dense mangroves with occasional shell-covered beaches, grateful for the outgoing tide gently towing our canoes, which are weighed down with camping gear, a watertight food bin, and five-gallon water jugs. On my nautical map, these isles, or keys, look like hundreds of single-celled organisms viewed through a powerful microscope. A labyrinth of channels weaves among them. Even the name Ten Thousand Islands inspires anxious visions of paddling in circles for days trying to distinguish Rabbit Key from Picnic Key from Jack Daniels Key from the scores of identical, thickly forested, shell-and-sand mounds that are simply labeled "mangrove" on the map, or not labeled at all.

As we look around, Penny says, "It would be really easy to get lost out here." I confess that I was thinking exactly the same thing.

The subtropical sun grills our necks and bare legs. Songbirds chatter and flit among the thick fur of trees along the shores. Cormorants and brown pelicans skim the water's surface. But no gators surreptitiously disguise themselves as driftwood out here; they stick to freshwater.

Beyond Indian Key Pass, the bay widens. Several canoes, private motorboats, and a couple of tour boats pass us; but mostly we are quite alone. We paddle around the tiny Stop Keys, at the outer edge of the islands, looking out over the emerald and infinite Gulf of Mexico.

I glance at Penny and Alex, sharing a canoe. Alex feigns an occasional paddle stroke—her MO. Penny smiles back at me. Her supremely relaxed expression speaks volumes about the therapeutic value of subtropical sun, beautiful scenery, and an escort from an air force of exotic birds. The kids point and laugh at silvery fish called mullets that leap high out of the ocean and nosedive back in.

Alex calls out, "Nate, do you agree this is the best trip? Better than the Olympic coast?" Nate considers this, saying he needs more time to render that judgment. This matter of rating our adventures over the past year on their own fun meter has become serious business to my kids. It reminds me that 329 days have ticked past since we started down the Grandview Trail into the Grand Canyon. Nate has turned ten, Alex is nearly eight, and they have now hiked, paddled, and skied through places whose names were not even part of my vocabulary at their ages.

As the tide recedes, the sea bottom rises, in places, to within inches of our hulls. Nate leans over our bow scouting for rocks and corals, calling to me, "Whoa! Whoa! Hard to port! Hard to starboard!" Still, Penny and I step out of our canoes to pull them through areas where the ocean is just ankle deep.

By late morning, we reach Tiger Key, another mangrove-covered rise of sand and crushed shells. We unload the canoes, hauling our gear in several trips across a hundred yards of tidal mudflats up onto a long, white-sand beach facing the open gulf, a beach we will have to ourselves for two days. Then we laboriously drag our empty canoes across the sandal-sucking mud.

The kids immediately set to the task of building "sand cities," fortifying them with walls against the irrepressible tide—constructing their statements of childish optimism. A few hours later, by midafternoon, Nate comes to me suggesting he and I take a canoe out exploring.

A strong breeze sends choppy, high-tide waves marching toward the beach. With only Nate's sixty pounds in the bow, it bounces like a basketball over the surf; he laughs as it leaps off each wave and slaps loudly onto the next. But once we enter a protected little bay, the wind abruptly disappears and the water flattens out.

Two ospreys land in a giant nest. A brown pelican cruises around the bay. As we drift lazily, Nate suddenly points and blurts out, "I just saw a dolphin! I saw the fin go up!"

Then we both see the fin and arched back rise and dive. We watch the dolphin head straight toward us. It surfaces again off our bow and dives beneath the canoe; we hear the dolphin inhale as it pops up behind us. "This is my favorite animal!" Nate says. For perhaps twenty minutes, we watch it swim laps around the bay, surfacing, blowing air, and diving, before it heads out to sea.

Nate relaxes his upper body, releases a long sigh, and sits quietly, as if he has just viewed the terrifying and glorious face of God. He remains silent for some minutes as we paddle back toward camp. Then my well-traveled young son tells me, "You know, Dad, thinking back on this past year, and all of these trips we've done, I think it might be my best year ever. I just think of how much fun all these trips were, and all the waypoints for me that this past year had, with all these different adventures."

Waypoints in the best year of a ten-year-old boy's life—there is some kind of nascent self-awareness in that immature perspective.

As Nate and I drag our canoe up onto our private wilderness beach, I notice that the waves have all but erased the kids' sand cities.

IMAGINE STIRRING A POT containing 300 million cubic miles of soup, and you have a vague grasp of the complexity of the Earth's oceans.

Sea level is not actually uniform around the globe; it varies due to differences in ocean circulation, gravitational pull, and minute shifts in the planet's rotational axis. Rising temperatures swell the oceans both through the melting of glaciers and ice caps, and through physics: since 1993, according to the IPCC, more than half of sea-level rise has been due to thermal expansion—seawater expanding as it warms.

The IPCC's 2007 report synthesis places this in perspective in stark, unambiguous terms: "Both past and future anthropogenic CO_2 emissions will continue to contribute to warming and sea level rise for more than a millennium, due to the time scales required for the removal of this gas from the atmosphere."

A millennium—a thousand years. At least forty human generations will wrestle with rising heat, rising oceans, rising ecological damage, and rising devastation to societies that was triggered by the actions and choices of just a few generations.

But the ocean's inexorable invasion of terminally flat South Florida represents merely the most conspicuous of a hotter climate's myriad effects on the Everglades.

"We're looking at [impacts on] birds, invertebrates, mammals, reptiles, fishes—just about everything," Leonard Pearlstine, the national park's landscape ecologist, told me.

The sea invading freshwater marshes will contaminate groundwater, damage prairie plants, and eliminate wildlife habitat. It could wipe out most of the park's pinelands. A June 2010 Park Service paper forecasted that a mere fifteen-inch rise in sea level will erase half of salt marshes, 60 percent of estuarine beaches, and most tidal flats in Gulf Coast areas like the Ten Thousand Islands. It bears repeating that fifteen inches represents less than half the minimum rise now expected.

As increasingly severe droughts magnify wildfires and shrink sinkholes where fish survive the winter dry season, wading birds will starve. The gender of reptile offspring, determined by temperatures during embryo incubation, may tip out of balance. Rare animals that live nowhere else will perish.

Florida Bay has the third-largest coral reef system in the world, stretching 150 miles from Key Biscayne to the Dry Tortugas. Rising seas inhibit coral growth by reducing sunlight reaching them. Sea-surface temperatures more than 3.6 degrees Fahrenheit (2 degrees Celsius) above normal cause "bleaching," in which corals eject symbiotic algae that give them their brilliant colors. In the hot summer of 2005, 80 percent of Caribbean corals surveyed showed bleaching; 40 percent died. Today, only about one-tenth of the Florida Keys reef consists of live corals. The IPCC predicts that sea-surface temperatures may rise by 3.6 degrees Fahrenheit (2 degrees Celsius) to 9 degrees Fahrenheit (5 degrees Celsius) in my kids' lifetimes. Meanwhile, rising acidification of the oceans threatens organisms that are the foundation of reefs.

"Unless we reverse our actions very quickly, by the end of the century, reefs could be a thing of the past," Ken Caldeira, a scientist with the Carnegie Institution and Stanford University, stated in a December 2007 article in *Science*.

But of all the ecological troubles hanging over the Everglades, scientists and park officials focus on one in particular. Many experts believe that the future of the Everglades ultimately rests on the backs—or roots—of the mangroves.

Mangroves provide habitat for a Noah's ark of birds, fish, mammals, reptiles, and amphibians. More important, their deep and intertwined root systems have, over eons, built up a sort of natural peat berm that shields inland freshwater marshes from the ocean. These tangled forests are the foundation of the ecosystem. And they are in danger.

Having evolved in a world with stable sea level, South Florida's mangroves have so far largely withstood sea-level rise of about 3 millimeters, or one-tenth of an inch, per year since the early 1990s (up from 2 millimeters per year through most of the twentieth century). Evidence also suggests that mangroves have accumulated fifteen feet of peat over the past 2,500 years, a long-term rate of six feet per thousand years.

But three-plus feet (one meter) of sea-level rise by 2100 would represent a tripling of the current rate; more than six feet (two meters) by 2100 means that mangroves would have to build up peat ten times faster than they have over more than two millennia, migrate inland, or face inundation by the ocean. A 2008 Park Service report predicted that, if the higher estimates of sea-level rise bear out, saltwater will overstep the mangrove berms in numerous places, stripping away peat down to limestone bedrock and creating the potential for "catastrophic inundation of South Florida."

"As rates of sea-level rise go up, it becomes very questionable whether [mangroves] are going to be able to keep up," Pearlstine, the park's landscape ecologist, told me.

Already, peat soils and mangroves have been lost in the Cape Sable area, partly because century-old canals allowed the ocean to penetrate freshwater marshes. As saw grass, pinelands, and other flora die and peat breaks down, they release carbon—another positive feedback fueling global warming.

A big hurricane can also crack open the mangrove fortress, and computer models show tropical storms growing more intense as the climate and ocean warm. In 2005, a record four of twenty-eight named Atlantic storms reached Category 5, the most powerful type of hurricane—including Wilma, the strongest Atlantic storm ever recorded, whose winds up to 185 mph caused sixty-two deaths and more than $16 billion in damage. Four major hurricanes hit Florida. An article in the journal *Science* that same year reported that the number of intense tropical storms has risen by a whopping 80 percent worldwide over the past thirty-five years.

Matt Patterson grew up in Florida, began SCUBA diving the 'Glades in the 1980s, served as a U.S. Navy submariner, and became a scientist in the mid-nineties. Now he coordinates the National Park Service's South Florida Caribbean Inventory & Monitoring Network, a team of scientists building a long-term ecosystem-monitoring program for seven national park units. He sees a rather grim future in which Everglades loses most of its freshwater marsh, the mangrove forests retreat far inland, coral reefs waste away, and big storms transform the Ten Thousand Islands into barren sandbars.

"I didn't think when I was studying marine science in the early to mid-nineties that my job would be this depressing," Patterson said to me. "It's rough watching the coral reefs that I love to dive on just disappearing before my eyes."

Then Patterson struck a chord that resonated with me, adding, "I have a ten- and thirteen-year-old and it frightens me to think things will be very different for them."

———

IN THE WHISPERING HOUR before dawn on our second day in the Ten Thousand Islands, with the low-tide stench of salt and shellfish hanging like butchered meat on the still air, dozens of white ibises high-step through shallow tide pools in the mudflats. Their heads bob up and down, stabbing into the water with slender, curved beaks. The ancient Egyptians believed the ibis was the reincarnation of Thoth, the god of wisdom and learning. Watching these birds, with beaks crafted by time and genetic serendipity to do one thing well—pluck crayfish from mud—it is easy to imagine them possessing some programmed, primordial knowledge that will always see them through.

The low-tide pools reflect a sky painted in muted colors: salmon, blue, soft browns and reds. Scores of a smaller bird that I do not recognize take flight from a sandbar. The birds dice the air with sharp, synchronized turns, rapidly flipping back and forth in unison between showing me their dark backs and their white bellies, evoking a few hundred mirrors spinning against the sky.

My family slumbers in our tent at the high end of the beach. Last night shortly after six o'clock, with waves plowing earnestly across the space now filled by acres of mudflats, we had all stood transfixed watching a star fall into the Gulf of Mexico. The sun, a swollen, hot coal, slipped torpidly across a deeply bloodshot sky. It drew out the silent drama of easing itself into the ocean—becoming a half-ball of fire, then a quarter-ball, then a bleeding sliver on a level, liquid horizon. And sunset will unfold like that every night we are in the Everglades.

By late morning, too antsy to wait for the ocean to come to us, we go to it—dragging the canoes across fifty yards of mud to the water. We circumnavigate Tiger Key, a three-hour expedition spent in part struggling against winds that spin the canoes.

"There are no other Everglades in the world. They are, they have always been, one of the unique regions of the earth; remote, never wholly known."

Those are the opening lines to *Everglades: River of Grass,* by Marjory Stoneman Douglas, published in 1947, the year Everglades National

Park was established. A champion of causes from feminism to racial justice, she fought much of her life to preserve the 'Glades. She understood, before many, that the myriad canals and levees outside the park were sickening the Everglades. Those lines may have been intended as a statement about the mysterious character of South Florida's flagship park, but they also prophesied the "never wholly known" future of El Laguno del Espiritu Santo.

In a 2010 report, Pearlstine made a statement that sounds simultaneously ominous yet optimistic. It reads, "Climate change and sea-level rise alone will not destroy the Everglades."

The regional Comprehensive Everglades Restoration Plan, or CERP, seeks to increase freshwater flow through Shark River and Taylor sloughs to Florida Bay by removing some canals and levees outside the park. The goal is, in essence, to push back against the rising ocean.

"It doesn't prevent sea-level rise. We're going to have to deal with that down the road," Stephen Davis, a wetlands ecologist with the Everglades Foundation, told me. "But this makes a more habitable Everglades ecosystem that has a capacity to support the species that are out there for as long as possible."

Pearlstine expressed to me a sentiment about the Everglades that I have heard from many other scientists and officials regarding our national parks.

"Part of what we need to do is accept change," Pearlstine said. "We may be looking at going from a mostly marsh-grassland system in Everglades National Park to an estuary, but we have to be careful about protecting our systems so that they have time to adapt."

In the afternoon of our second day on Tiger Key, with the high tide sloshing boisterously onto the beach, Alex comes to me wanting a father-daughter paddle. Penny is content to hang out with her book, and Nate to continue fortifying his doomed sand city. So my seven-year-old girl and I bounce over the choppy waves, around the island's arm into that protected little bay—and then through a hidden, fifty-foot-long mangrove tunnel into a small lagoon that we all explored on our paddle around Tiger Key.

Alex and I want to see whether ten roseate spoonbills are still in the bare branches of a dead tree on the lagoon's shore. The four of us had earlier spotted the large, flamboyantly all-pink wading birds, which get their color from a pigment found in crustaceans they eat.

As we slowly round a bend in the lagoon's shoreline, Alex, in the bow, turns around to me with a big smile and whispers, "They're still there!"

Two of the spoonbills fly over us and then circle back to the tree. Alex and I sit, barely stirring, maybe fifty feet from the birds, watching them through binoculars. She keeps glancing and grinning at me, as if we have somehow stepped into the pages of her favorite fairy tale and she cannot believe we are here among these unreal characters.

After an Audubon Society researcher found just two spoonbill nests in all of Florida Bay in 1936, recovery efforts built their numbers up to 1,200 by 1980. But the local population has been in decline for several years. Pete Frezza, research manager with the Florida Audubon Society Tavernier Science Center, told me that field workers counted just sixty-five nests in the park this year, the lowest number since 1952. No one understands why spoonbills are leaving a million and a half acres of protected national park to nest elsewhere in Florida. "Something's going on in Florida Bay, and we don't know what," Frezza said. "It's perplexing."

I don't tell Alex the roseate spoonbill's mercurial story; I don't want to do anything to disturb our moment. All the efforts to protect natural reserves and vulnerable species are partly about preserving experiences like this one, when a parent and child can share a big drink from the cup of wonder and remember the taste for the rest of their lives.

If Alex and Nate someday they tell their own children or grandchildren about this trip, it may sound like the myth of Atlantis.

Arguably more than with any other national park, retaining a sense of hope for the Everglades demands a deep and abiding optimism that is hard to call up. It could become a poignant symbol of the failures of modern civilization—or restoration could succeed, at least partly. Some of the mangroves could hold up. The Everglades could stand as an inspirational symbol of our ability to do what's difficult, but necessary and right.

If the future of the 'Glades seems to hang on the thinnest thread of hope, this vast, flat marsh reminds us of something fundamental to our humanity: without hope, we have nothing. Just as a parent does what is needed for his or her children, we have no better alternative to preserving our world. Giving up on hope is giving up on tomorrow.

After perhaps fifteen minutes, I ask Alex whether we should leave the spoonbills alone now. She agrees. We paddle back through the mangrove portal, and back over the choppy surf to our campsite, where Alex breathlessly regales Penny and Nate with the details of our sighting, just as Nate had yesterday with the dolphin.

Hope cannot alter topography and it cannot hold back the sea. There is no avoiding a certain harsh reality of a flat continental appendage and a rising ocean.

But maybe, like the white ibis foraging for crayfish in the mudflats at low tide, my kids will tap into some well of knowledge to help them survive in the remade world of the twenty-first century. Maybe they are filling that well with knowledge acquired on our wilderness ramblings of the past twelve months.

For the sake of my children, I embrace optimism.

EPILOGUE

I set out in the past year to show my kids glaciers before they disappear, wild coasts doomed to sink below the waves, and the world's grandest canyon before rising temperatures and aridity make it less hospitable. I hoped they might at least partly internalize the deeper meaning of waterfalls, forests, and winter diminishing in their lifetimes.

But mostly, they saw other things.

The memories likely to stay with them will be of a young mountain goat barring our trail, a city of mussels and sea anemones clinging to a boulder at low tide, a dolphin swimming circles around our canoe, roseate spoonbills filling a tree, and the jolt to the senses of encountering seals, bison, alligators, and a brown bear's paw print. They will remember sliding down snowfields in summer, building driftwood battleships, and the creeks, tide pools, and beaches where they passed hours imagining other worlds. They will tell stories of crossing a swaying bridge over a river gray and roaring, singing Christmas songs in falling snow, and laughingly hurling sticks into a swift current.

We can only expose children to experiences that etch lasting memories; they will chart the journey of learning from there.

But I believe Nate and Alex have also absorbed some of the larger lessons I tried to impart. Someday, they will look back on this year through the lens of adult perspective and see our adventures more as I do: as moments that cannot be repeated because they were rooted deeply in a specific time in their lives, shared in places of unmatched singularity that cannot remain the same.

Alex and Nate will understand then that I wanted to take these trips with them before these park experiences are gone or greatly changed—but also, before the two of them are grown and gone.

AN UNANTICIPATED COINCIDENCE PARALLELED our travels: 2010, when most of our national park adventures took place, tied 2005 as the hottest year worldwide since record keeping began in the nineteenth century, according to the National Oceanic and Atmospheric Administration and the U.N.'s World Meteorological Organization.

New York City endured its hottest summer ever and Los Angeles hit 113 degrees Fahrenheit for the first time on September 27. Arctic sea-ice cover reached a new low. The Atlantic hurricane season was the third-most active of the past century. The 950 natural disasters in 2010 significantly exceeded the ten-year average of 785, according to the multinational reinsurance company Munich Re's annual report on disasters; more to the point, 90 percent of them were weather-related, including the heat wave and wildfires in Russia that killed 56,000 and floods in Pakistan that left *twenty-six million people* homeless.

Erratic, destructive weather seems to have become the norm in recent years. In November 2010, Minnesota farmer Jack Hedin wrote in an op-ed piece in the *New York Times*:

> The past four years of heavy rains and flash flooding here in southern Minnesota have left me worried about the future of agriculture in America's grain belt. For some time computer models of climate change have been predicting just these kinds of weather patterns, but seeing them unfold on our farm has been harrowing nonetheless. . . . In August 2007, a series of storms produced a breathtaking 23 inches of rain in 36 hours. The flooding essentially erased our farm from the map. The more than 20 inches of rain that I measured in my rain gauge in June and July [2010] disrupted nearly every operation on our farm. . . . [N]o fewer than three "thousand-year rains" have occurred in the past seven years.

And the ten warmest years on record have all occurred since 1998. Yet, we continue heading in the wrong direction. The year 2010 was also notable for humanity's setting a record for carbon dioxide emissions, pouring 30.6 gigatons into the atmosphere, according to the International Energy Agency. That news prompted the IEA's chief economist, Fatih Birol, to call the goal of keeping the average global temperature increase within 2 degrees Celsius (3.6 degrees Fahrenheit)—the threshold beyond which many scientists fear Earth will spiral into catastrophic climate change—merely "a nice utopia." Experts widely suspect that warming of 3 to 4 degrees Celsius (5.4 to 7.2 degrees Fahrenheit) is virtually inevitable in coming decades. At that point, the Amazon transforms to desert and grasslands and burns, the Greenland and West Antarctic ice sheets collapse, a third of all species become extinct, and drought conditions of historic proportions become common—not to mention epic famine and refugee crises. All as the world continues getting hotter.

Meanwhile, world energy demand will grow by more than one-third over the next twenty-five years, the IEA projected in November 2010.

Almost every scientist I interviewed for this book offered the same caveat: predicting the future is risky business. And yet, the same scientists, almost to a person, voiced a sense of dread for what awaits us. And they're not talking about the distant future; they're talking about ecological calamities and social breakdown on a scale unprecedented in human history, which many adults alive today will witness.

Many echoed the comments of USGS research ecologist Nathan Stephenson, who told me, "Sometimes people say, 'If this has happened in the past, why should we be worried?' The simple answer is, you would not have wanted to be alive then. Civilizations have fallen on slight changes in climate."

The emotional weight of it all is crushing.

At the same time, what USGS biologist Dan Fagre said to me about Glacier National Park rings true of all these places: "It's still going to be a beautiful park. The notion that it's being changed ultimately by human activities is something people have to take responsibility for. These are really good things for people to be thinking about."

When I interviewed National Park Service director Jon Jarvis, he spoke of his hope for growing public support for governmental and international efforts to mitigate climate change being inspired by "the love affair that Americans have with their national parks—which is very strong. My goal is for the public to understand that there are significant effects happening in the parks right now. The role for the national parks is to tell the American story, good and bad, and learn from it."

Jarvis added, "We're not going to stop climate change tomorrow, but we can help slow it down, adapt, lead the world, and preserve these extraordinary places."

So we face the question: are we willing to change our behavior not only for our parks, but for our children?

Our conversation about climate has not achieved the degree of honesty we would use when talking with our own kids. We would not encourage them to make choices fraught with such a high degree of risk. Yet we as a people have embraced just that kind of choice time and again.

The leading carbon-producing nations quibble over how much each should be allowed to continue degrading our shared house. The venerable United States Senate has members who question the existence of climate change. The Republican Party openly espouses policies based in uninformed populism instead of science. A 2010 *New York Times* editorial pointed out that some twenty GOP candidates for the U.S. Senate did not "accept the scientific consensus that humans are largely responsible for global warming."

But sadly, Congress does, to some extent, mirror the views of voters. The Pew Research Center reported in June 2011 that fewer than 60 percent of Americans "believed in" global warming, compared with 77 percent five years earlier—and only one-third of Americans attributed climate change to carbon emissions.

We continue struggling for answers to the wrong questions. Asking whether a particular hurricane or heat wave is a direct consequence of climate change cannot produce a useful answer. We should be asking, Is this weather event precisely what has been predicted as a result of warming? Almost always, the answer is "yes," and that should dictate how we respond, not the minute uncertainty over cause.

Humans possess great adaptability. But applying that ability begins with acknowledging the truth. Failing to be honest with ourselves is tantamount to lying to our children.

In one generation, we changed attitudes in America toward smoking cigarettes , driving while intoxicated, and wearing seatbelts—in part because we recognized that changing our behaviors was a demonstration of love and caring for our children. Driving less, reducing energy consumption at home and work, and demanding that our leaders support converting from fossil fuels to clean energy—these are a powerful expression of concern for our kids.

Climate change forces us to confront our deepest values, to decide what's most important to us.

HOW DOES THIS STORY end? It doesn't—not this year, anyway. It continues with me involved, hopefully for quite a while yet, and with more adventures, and with my children growing up in a world very different from the one I grew up in.

I imagine a final chapter, years from now.

An adult stands silently at a mountain pass, or on a wild beach or a patch of desert, or bobs in a kayak or a canoe in waters far removed from civilization. Although this person has been here before, it looks only vaguely recognizable. Memory distorts reality, of course, but there is no doubt this place has undergone dramatic change since he or she visited years ago. Perhaps the sea presses in where it did not exist before; or dirt and a mangy mat of some pernicious weed from Asia have replaced age-old ice; or a kind of sterilization has eradicated many of the animals and plants that once thrived here, leaving only the wilderness equivalents of rats and dandelions. The scene evokes for this person the sensation of standing in a former home that has been looted of most of its furniture and valuables. The wind still blows, but it's hotter than this person remembers. There is less natural sound, too, replaced by the echo of emptiness.

The place still retains some official designation heralding it as a spot of special natural importance. But that long ago became a bitter joke among people who knew its former condition.

This person summons a childhood recollection of laughingly sliding on skis with family over this ground that's now bare in February, or playing by a creek that has dried up in June, or hiking a trail engaged for hours in a conversation about something that could only engage a child. Especially in this degraded world, those memories are worth very much.

Recalling moments of joy, curiosity, and wonder, he or she may shed a tear salted with both disappointment and happiness, curse in anger and frustration, and contemplate what was and what might have been.

But that's not the ending I would write.

In my preferred closing scene, this person feels both melancholy and appreciation, because while much has changed, a far greater disaster was averted. Humanity rose to the challenges it faced. People and nations willingly sacrificed and adapted.

Someday this story's ending will be written, and our children will know which scene turned out to be imaginary and which has become their reality.

ACKNOWLEDGMENTS

I am deeply grateful to my agent, Gary Heidt of Signature Literary Agency, for his willingness to take on an unknown writer with an offbeat idea and work hard to land me a contract. Any writer, new or established, would do well to enlist his services.

From my first, long conversation with my editor at Beacon Press, Alexis Rizzuto, I realized that I had what every aspiring author dreams of: a contract with a respected publisher and an editor I immediately liked. Over the course of more than a year, as I worked on this book, Alexis demonstrated that she possesses the skill to make my writing better and the humility to recognize when she had done enough. I'm doubly fortunate to have made a new friend. I will have to concoct excuses to chat with her once in a while now that this book is done.

Family members and friends joined us on several adventures, making those experiences more memorable and reminding all of us how much richer our interactions are in the wilderness, where there's no entertainment but conversation. Our companions included my mother, Joanne Lanza; my nephew Marco Garofalo; my brother-in-law Tom Beach and his son Daniel; Jon, Heather, Hadley, and Abby Dorn; Larry Geis; Bill Mistretta and Jenna Berman; and Jeff Wilhelm and his daughter Jasmine.

A story is often shaped by the input of many people, and I owe a debt of gratitude to several who read and advised me on portions of this book, including Michael Hannigan, Rod Venterea, Doug Shinneman, my sister Julie Lanza, and my wife, Penny Beach, but especially to two good friends who read and advised me on nearly every chapter, Mark Godley and Jeff Wilhelm. The feedback from all of them helped improve this story.

I would be remiss if I did not express my gratitude to the many brilliant and accomplished scientists and authorities on climate change who selflessly gave of their time to answer my many questions, all of whom are listed in the Sources section of this book.

While planning wilderness adventures in the only two parks that I had not previously visited, I tapped into the knowledge of people who know these places the best. Alaska Mountain Guides & Climbing School generously hosted my family on a sea kayaking trip in Glacier Bay National Park, and our guides, Sarah Rennick and Dan Berk, made it fun and safe. Justin Shurr of Shurr Adventures patiently responded to my numerous e-mails over the several months leading up to our Everglades visit and provided on-the-ground support and guiding. I feel deep gratitude for how much he did to enable that trip and great respect for his intimate knowledge of an environment that so fiercely eludes knowing.

Several organizations and companies supported my travels in various ways, and I want to thank State of Alaska Tourism; the Alpine Inn at Crystal Mountain, Washington; the Colorado Tourism Office; Grace Haven Retreat in Rockport, Washington; Huckleberry Lodge in Forks, Washington; the Olympic Peninsula Visitor Bureau; Washington State Tourism; and Xanterra Parks & Resorts.

I have saved for last the three people without whom this story could not have been told. My wife, Penny, was unfailingly supportive, including placing unbelievable trust in my judgments to take our young kids on adventures that carried some real risks. Although she wavered a bit when it came to kayaking among alligators, I love her and appreciate her understanding—not to mention her ability to carry a heavy backpack.

And, of course, this story would be vastly less colorful without our son, Nate, and daughter, Alex, two smart, enthusiastic, and creative people who make me infinitely proud and demonstrate time and again that kids are capable of far more than adults tend to believe. My kids have surely taught me more in the past ten years than I learned in the previous forty.

SOURCES

PROLOGUE: INSPIRATION

International Union for Conservation of Nature (IUCN), Red List of Threatened Species, "Extinction Crisis Continues Apace," November 3, 2009, www.iucn .org/.

"Matterhorn Declared Off-Limits to Climbers," Swissinfo, July 16, 2003, http:// www.swissinfo.ch/.

United Nations Educational, Scientific and Cultural Organization (UNESCO), World Heritage List, http://whc.unesco.org/.

CHAPTER 1: DEEPEST EARTH

Carl Bowman, "Air and Rock: Changing Climates at Grand Canyon," Grand Canyon National Park Division of Interpretation & Resource Education report.

Kenneth L. Cole, "Vegetation Response to Early Holocene Warming as an Analog for Current and Future Changes," *Conservation Biology* 24, no. 1 (2009): 29–37.

Grand Canyon Association, "Quest for the Pillar of Gold," chapter 2, www.grand canyon.org/.

Grand Canyon National Park, "Nature & Science" and "A Study of Seeps and Springs," www.nps.gov/.

Andrew C. Revkin, "Weird Weather in a Warming World," *Dot Earth* blog, *New York Times,* September 7, 2010.

Steve Rice, "Native Waters: Springs and Seeps," parts 1, 2, and 3, YouTube, www .youtube.com/.

Stephen Saunders, Charles Montgomery, Tom Easley, and Theo Spencer, "Hotter and Drier—The West's Changed Climate," Rocky Mountain Climate Organization and Natural Resources Defense Council, March 2008, www.rocky mountainclimate.org/.

University Corporation for Atmospheric Research (UCAR), "Climate Change: Drought May Threaten Much of Globe within Decades," October 19, 2010, www2.ucar.edu/.

Wikipedia, "Geology of the Grand Canyon Area," "Grand Canyon Weather," "History of the Grand Canyon Area," and "National Monument (United States)," http://en.wikipedia.org/.

George P. Winship, "The Coronado Expedition, 1540–1542," *U.S. Bureau of Ethnology, 14th Annual Report, Part 1,* translations of the Relacion de Suceso.

The author conducted interviews for this chapter with the following:

Kenneth L. Cole, research professor, Northern Arizona University, retired research ecologist, paleoecologist, and climate scientist, USGS Colorado Plateau Research Station.

Richard Quartaroli, Cline Library Special Collections librarian, Northern Arizona University.

CHAPTER 2: HOW DOES THE WATER GO UP THE MOUNTAIN?

Leonard Anderson, "Climate Change Threatens California Water Supply," *Reuters,* May 9, 2007, www.reuters.com/.

California Department of Water Resources, "California Water Plan Update 2005," www.waterplan.water.ca.gov/.

————. "Climate Change," www.water.ca.gov/.

Michael D. Dettinger, Daniel R. Cayan, Noah Knowles, Anthony Westerling, and Mary K. Tyree, "Recent Projections of 21st-Century Climate Change and Watershed Responses in the Sierra Nevada," paper, Sierra Nevada Science Symposium, October 7–10, 2002, Kings Beach, CA.

Bill McKibben, *Eaarth* (New York: Henry Holt and Company, 2010).

Mary Milliken, "Water Scarcity Clouds California Farming's Future," *Reuters,* March 13, 2009, www.reuters.com/.

Craig Moritz et al., "Impact of a Century of Climate Change on Small-Mammal Communities in Yosemite National Park, USA," *Science* 322, no. 5899 (2008): 261–64.

Philip W. Mote, "Climate-Driven Variability and Trends in Mountain Snowpack in Western North America," *Journal of Climate* 19 (2006): 6209–20.

National Park Service, "Climate Change in National Parks," www.nps.gov/.

Sierra Nevada Virtual Museum, "Sierra Snowfall Records," www.sierranevadavirtualmuseum.com/.

Matt Walker, "Warming 'Big Threat' to Yosemite," BBC Earth News, November 2, 2009, http://news.bbc.co.uk/.

Wikipedia. "Merced River" and "Yosemite Falls," http://en.wikipedia.org/.

Yosemite National Park, "Plants," "Study the Scientist: A Hydrologist," "Vegetation Species List," and "Waterfalls." www.nps.gov/.

The author conducted interviews for this chapter with the following:

Kari Cobb, Yosemite National Park Information Office.

Michael D. Dettinger, research hydrologist, Branch of Western Regional Research, U.S. Geological Survey, and research associate, Climate, Atmospheric Sciences and Physical Oceanography Division, Scripps Institution of Oceanography.

Philip Mote, director, Oregon Climate Change Research Institute and Oregon Climate Services, College of Oceanic and Atmospheric Sciences, Oregon State University, Corvallis.

Jon Riedel, geologist and principal investigator, Glacier Monitoring Program, North Cascades National Park, Marblemount, WA.

Greg Stock, geologist, Yosemite National Park.

Steve Thompson, wildlife biologist, branch chief, Wildlife Management, Division of Resources Management & Science, Yosemite National Park.

CHAPTER 3: THE DISTANT RUMBLE OF WHITE THUNDER

Alister Doyle, "Ocean Acidification May Threaten Food Security: U.N.," *Reuters,* December 2, 2010, www.reuters.com/.

Glacier Bay National Park and Preserve. "An Overview of Selected Glaciers in Glacier Bay," "Change," "Coasts/Shorelines," "Glaciers/Glacial Features," "Harbor Seal Research," "Intertidal and Subtidal Zones," "Natural History of Glacier Bay," "Oceanography," and "Plant Communities," www.nps.gov/.

Kim Heacox, *The Only Kayak* (Guilford, CT: Lyons Press, 2005).

Bill McKibben, *Eaarth* (New York: Henry Holt, 2010).

Fen Montaigne, "The Warming of Antarctica: A Citadel of Ice Begins to Melt," *Yale Environment 360,* November 22, 2010, http://e360.yale.edu/.

Roman J. Motyka et al., "Post Little Ice Age Rebound in the Glacier Bay Region," *Proceedings of the Fourth Glacier Bay Science Symposium,* National Park Service, October 2004, www.nps.gov/.

NASA Earth Observatory, "Jakobshavn Glacier Retreat," July 15, 2010, http://earthobservatory.nasa.gov/.

National Snow and Ice Data Center, "Sea Ice," http://nsidc.org/.

Norway Ministry of Foreign Affairs, "Foreign Minister Støre and Former Vice President Al Gore Present Report on Melting Ice at Climate Summit," December 14, 2009, www.regjeringen.no/.

TravelJuneau.com, "Bird's Eye View: Spring Bird Migration," www.traveljuneau.com/.

University of Bristol, "Greenland Ice Cap Melting Faster Than Ever," *ScienceDaily,* November 13, 2009, www.sciencedaily.com/.

Fabian Walter et al., "Iceberg Calving during Transition from Grounded to Floating Ice: Columbia Glacier, Alaska," *Geophysical Research Letters* 37 (2010): 1–4.

Wikipedia, "Glacier Bay National Park and Preserve" and "Post-Glacial Rebound," http://en.wikipedia.org/.

The author conducted interviews for this chapter with the following:

Christine Gabriele, whale biologist, Glacier Bay National Park and Preserve.

Bruce Molnia, research geologist, U.S. Geological Survey.

Sue Moore, research scientist, Fisheries Office of Science and Technology, National Oceanic and Atmospheric Administration.

Brendan Moynahan, program manager, Southeast Alaska Network, National Park Service Inventory and Monitoring Program.

Tad Pfeffer, professor and North American glacier expert, Institute of Arctic and Alpine Research (INSTAAR), University of Colorado, Boulder.

Chad Soiseth, fisheries biologist, Glacier Bay National Park and Preserve.

Jamie Womble, wildlife biologist, National Park Service.

CHAPTER 4: IN THE LONG SHADOW OF "THE MOUNTAIN"

Climate Impacts Group, University of Washington, "Climate Change," March 2008, http://cses.washington.edu/.

Michael D. Dettinger, "Climate Change, Atmospheric Rivers, and Future California Floods," paper, Extreme Precipitation Symposium, Sacramento, CA, June 24, 2009, http://cepsym.info/.

Jack Hedin, "An Almanac of Extreme Weather," *New York Times,* November 27, 2010.

Mt. Rainier National Park, "Frequently Asked Questions," "Nature & Science," and "November 2006 Flooding," www.nps.gov/.

Andrew C. Revkin, "Scientists See Links from Asian Floods to Russian Heat," *Dot Earth* blog, *New York Times,* August 10, 2010.

Wikipedia, "Cascade Volcanoes," "Glacial Lake Outburst Flood," "Lahar," and "Mount Rainier," http://en.wikipedia.org/.

The author conducted interviews for this chapter with the following:

Kevin Bacher, volunteer manager, Mt. Rainier National Park.

Carl Fabiani, trails foreman, Mt. Rainier National Park.

Paul Kennard, regional geomorphologist, Pacific Northwest Region, National Park Service.

Anne Nolin, climatologist and assistant professor, Department of Geosciences, Oregon State University, Corvallis.

Dave Uberuaga, superintendent, Mt. Rainier National Park.

CHAPTER 5: ALONG A WILD COAST

Climate Impacts Group, University of Washington, "Climate Impacts on Pacific Northwest Coasts," http://cses.washington.edu/.

Kai Huschke, *Washington's Wilderness Areas* (Englewood, CO: Westcliffe Publishers, 2003).

Philip Mote, Alexander Petersen, Spencer Reeder, Hugh Shipman, and Lara Whitely Binder, *Sea Level Rise in the Coastal Waters of Washington State,* University of Washington Climate Impacts Group and the Washington Department of Ecology, January 2008, p. 9.

National Oceanic and Atmospheric Administration, "Scientists Find 20 Years of Deep Water Warming Leading to Sea Level Rise," September 20, 2010, www.noaanews.noaa.gov/.

Olympic Coast National Marine Sanctuary, "History and Culture," September 8, 2005, http://olympiccoast.noaa.gov/.

Olympic National Park, "Temperate Rain Forests," www.nps.gov/.

————. Information page, www.olympic.national-park.com/.

Elizabeth A. Pendleton, Erika S. Hammar-Klose, E. Robert Thieler, and S. Jeffress Williams, "Coastal Vulnerability Assessment of Olympic National Park to Sea-Level Rise," U.S. Geological Survey open-file report 04–1021, electronic book (2004): 2–11.

United Nations Educational, Scientific and Cultural Organization (UNESCO), "Olympic National Park," World Heritage Convention, http://whc.unesco.org/.

University of Washington Glaciology Group, "Recent Climate Changes in Western Washington," www.ess.washington.edu/.

Wikipedia, "El Niño-Southern Oscillation" and "Olympic Coast National Marine Sanctuary," http://en.wikipedia.org/.

The author conducted interviews for this chapter with the following:

Bill Baccus, physical scientist, Olympic National Park.

Sam Brinkman, fisheries biologist, Olympic National Park.

Dave Conca, archeologist, Olympic National Park.

Steven Fradkin, coastal ecologist, Olympic National Park.

Suzanne Griffin, researcher of Olympic marmots.

Anne Nolin, climatologist and assistant professor, Department of Geosciences, Oregon State University, Corvallis.

CHAPTER 6: THE BACKBONE OF THE WORLD

Defenders of Wildlife, "Grizzly Bear," www.defenders.org/.

Glacier National Park, "Geologic Formations," "Mammals," "Nature & Science," and "Rivers and Streams," www.nps.gov/.

Jason D. B. Kauffman, "The Peak: Triple Divide Peak, Glacier National Park," *Backpacker,* September 2010, www.backpacker.com/.

Stephen Saunders, Tom Easley, and Theo Spencer; Rocky Mountain Climate Organization and Natural Resources Defense Council, "Glacier National Park in Peril—The Threats of Climate Disruption," April 2010, www.rockymountainclimate.org/.

U.S. Geological Survey Northern Rocky Mountain Science Center, "Glacier Moni-toring Studies" and "Retreat of Glaciers in Glacier National Park," www.nrmsc.usgs.gov/.

U.S. Geological Survey Office of Communication, "Rare Alpine Insect May Disap-pear with Glaciers," April 4, 2011, www.usgs.gov/.

Wikipedia, "Grinnell Glacier," http://en.wikipedia.org/.

The author conducted interviews for this chapter with the following:

Daniel B. Fagre, biologist and program coordinator, U.S. Geological Survey North-ern Rocky Mountain Science Center, Glacier Field Station, West Glacier, MT.

Mauri Pelto, director, North Cascades Glacier Climate Project, Nichols College, Dudley, MA.

Jack Potter, chief of science and resources management, Glacier National Park.

CHAPTER 7: IF A TREE FALLS

Barbara J. Bentz et al., "Climate Change and Bark Beetles of the Western United States and Canada: Direct and Indirect Effects," *BioScience* 60 (2010): 602–13.

British Columbia Ministry of Forests, Lands, and Natural Resource Operations, "Beetle Facts," www.for.gov.bc.ca/.

Colorado State Forest Service, "Colorado's Forest Types—Aspen" and "Colorado's Forest Types—Lodgepole Pine," http://csfs.colostate.edu/.

Lauren Glendenning, "Vail, Beaver Creek Take On Pine Beetle," *Vail (CO) Daily,* August 5, 2010, www.vaildaily.com/.

Robert E. Keane and Russell A. Parsons, "Restoring Whitebark Pine Forests of the Northern Rocky Mountains, USA," *Ecological Restoration* 28, no. 1 (March 2010): 56–70.

D. A. Leatherman, I. Aguayo, and T. M. Mehall, "Mountain Pine Beetle," fact sheet, no. 5.528, Colorado State University Extension, www.ext.colostate.edu/.

Staci Matlock, "Mysterious Condition Hits Aspens in West," *Santa Fe New Mexican,* September 20, 2009, www.santafenewmexican.com/.

Constance I. Millar, Nathan L. Stephenson, and Scott L. Stephens, "Climate Change and Forests of the Future: Managing in the Face of Uncertainty," *Eco-logical Applications* 17, no. 8 (2007): 2145–51.

Dana L. Perkins, "Ecology," Whitebark Pine Ecosystem Foundation, www.whitebarkfound.org/.

G. E. Rehfeldt, Dennis E. Ferguson, and Nicholas L. Crookston, "Aspen, Climate, and Sudden Decline in Western USA," *Forest Ecology and Management* 258 (2009): 2353–64.

Jim Robbins, "Old Trees May Soon Meet Their Match," *New York Times,* September 27, 2010.

Rocky Mountain National Park, "Aspen Beauty," fact sheet, May 2009, www.nps.gov/.

John W. Schwandt, "Whitebark Pine in Peril: A Rangewide Assessment and Strategies for Restoration," U.S. Forest Service Northern Region, 2007, http://www.fs.usda.gov.

Diana F. Tomback, "Whitebark Pine: Ecological Importance and Future Outlook," *Proceedings of the Conference: Whitebark Pine: A Pacific Coast Perspective,* 2007.

U.S. Forest Service, Rocky Mountain Region, "Rocky Mountain Region Forest Health Conditions, 2006–2008."

———. "Sudden Aspen Decline in Colorado," February 2009.

U.S. Forest Service Rocky Mountain Research Station, "Frequently Asked Questions About Mountain Pine Beetles in Colorado," www.fs.fed.us/rmrs/.

Utah State University, "Lodgepole Pine," http://extension.usu.edu/.

Matt Walker, "Yosemite's Giant Trees Disappear," BBC Earth News, May 22, 2009, http://news.bbc.co.uk/.

Wikipedia, "Aspen," http://en.wikipedia.org/.

James J. Worrall et al., "Effects and Etiology of Sudden Aspen Decline in Southwestern Colorado, USA," *Forest Ecology and Management* 260 (2010): 638–48.

The author conducted interviews for this chapter with the following:

Gretchen Baker, ecologist, Great Basin National Park, Baker, NV.

Barbara Bentz, research entomologist, U.S. Forest Service Rocky Mountain Research Station, Logan, UT.

Dan Binkley, professor of forest ecology, Department of Forest, Rangeland, and Watershed Stewardship, Warner College of Natural Resources, Fort Collins, CO.

José Negrón, research entomologist, U.S. Forest Service Rocky Mountain Research Station, Fort Collins, CO.

Bill Romme, professor, Department of Forest, Rangeland, and Watershed Stewardship, Colorado State University, Fort Collins, CO.

Stephen Saunders, president, Rocky Mountain Climate Organization, Louisville, CO.

Nathan Stephenson, research ecologist, Sequoia and Kings Canyon Field Station, U.S. Geological Survey Western Ecological Research Center, Three Rivers, CA.

Judy Visty, research administrator/ecologist, Continental Divide Research Learning Center, Rocky Mountain National Park.

CHAPTER 8: SEARCHING FOR DR. SEUSS

Cameron W. Barrows and Michelle L. Murphy, "Modeled Shifts in the Distribution of Vegetation Resulting from Climate Change Simulations within Joshua Tree National Park," University of California–Riverside Center for Conservation Biology, March 2011.

C. W. Barrows, "Sensitivity to Climate Change for Two Reptiles at the Mojave-Sonoran Desert Interface," *Journal of Arid Environments* 75 (2011): 629–35.

Kenneth L. Cole et al., "Past and Ongoing Shifts in Joshua Tree Support Future Modeled Range Contraction," *Ecological Applications* 21 (2011): 137–49.

James W. Cornett, "Giant Joshua Trees," *San Bernardino County Museum Association Quarterly* 44, no. 1 (1997): 30–31.

———. "Population Dynamics of the Joshua Tree (*Yucca brevifolia*): Twenty Year Analysis, Upper Covington Flat, Joshua Tree National Park," California State University, Desert Studies Consortium, abstracts from the 2009 Desert Symposium.

Theodor (Dr. Seuss) Geisel, *The Lorax* (New York: Random House, 1971).

Joshua Tree National Park, "Cacti/Desert Succulents," "Creosote Bush," "Joshua Trees," "Nature & Science," and "Rock Climbing," www.nps.gov/.

National Park Service, "Climate Change in National Parks," www.nps.gov/.

Camille Parmesan and Gary Yohe, "A Globally Coherent Fingerprint of Climate Change Impacts across Natural Systems," *Nature* 421, no. 2 (2003): 37–42.

Wikipedia, "Mojave Desert" and "*Yucca brevifolia,*" http://en.wikipedia.org/.

The author conducted interviews for this chapter with the following:

Cameron Barrows, assistant research ecologist, Desert Studies Initiative, Center for Conservation Biology, University of California–Riverside, Palm Desert, CA.

Kenneth L. Cole, research professor, Northern Arizona University, retired research ecologist, paleoecologist, and climate scientist, USGS Colorado Plateau Research Station.

James Cornett, desert ecologist, retired director and curator of natural sciences, Palm Springs Desert Museum, instructor at University of California–Riverside, Palm Springs, CA.

Todd Esque, research scientist, U.S. Geological Survey Western Ecological Resource Center, Las Vegas Field Station, Henderson, NV.

Joe Zarki, spokesman, Joshua Tree National Park.

CHAPTER 9: THE END OF WINTER

Matthew Brown, "Grizzly Bear Deaths in 2010 Near Record Levels Around Yellowstone," *Huffington Post,* December 30, 2010, www.huffingtonpost.com/.

Julia Cart, "Grim Outlook for Grizzlies in Yellowstone Region," *Los Angeles Times,* November 6, 2010.

Tim Flannery, *The Eternal Frontier—An Ecological History of North America and Its Peoples* (Melbourne, Australia: Text Publishing, 2001).

Glacier National Park, "Birds," www.nps.gov/.

Greater Yellowstone Science Learning Center, "Whitebark Pine," www.greateryellowstonescience.org/.

Greater Yellowstone Whitebark Pine Monitoring Working Group; C. C. Schwartz, M. A. Haroldson, and K. West, eds., *Monitoring Whitebark Pine in the Greater Yellowstone Ecosystem: 2009 Annual Report,* appendix B.

Interagency Grizzly Bear Committee, *Yellowstone Grizzly Bear Investigations: Annual Report 2010*, U.S. Geological Survey, Bozeman, MT.

———. "Yellowstone Ecosystem," www.igbconline.org/.

Intergovernmental Panel on Climate Change, "Climate Change 2007: Synthesis Report."

Robert E. Keane and Russell A. Parsons, "Restoring Whitebark Pine Forests of the Northern Rocky Mountains, USA," *Ecological Restoration* 28, no. 1 (March 2010): 56–70.

Brian Kevin, "Everybody Hates Chuck Schwartz," *Sierra*, January/February 2011, www.sierraclub.org/.

Todd M. Koel et al., "Yellowstone Fisheries & Aquatic Sciences Annual Report, 2007," Yellowstone Center for Resources, Yellowstone National Park, 2007.

Natural Resources Defense Council. "New Science Shows the Extent of Dying Whitebark Pine," www.nrdc.org/.

Elisabeth Rosenthal, "For Many Species, No Escape as Temperature Rises," *New York Times*, January 21, 2011.

Kim Sager, "Whitebark Pine Seeds, Red Squirrels, and Grizzly Bears: An Interconnected Relationship," BEHAVE—Behavioral Education for Human, Animal, Vegetation and Ecosystem Management, www.cnr.uidaho.edu/.

Daniel A. Shaw, "Global Warming Pushes Ski Industry Downhill," *Grist*, February 9, 2006.

Diana F. Tomback, "Whitebark Pine: Ecological Importance and Future Outlook," *Proceedings of the Conference: Whitebark Pine: A Pacific Coast Perspective*, 2007.

U.S. Geological Survey Northern Rocky Mountain Science Center, "Whitebark Pine Communities," www.nrmsc.usgs.gov/.

Anthony L. Westerling et al., "Continued Warming Could Transform Greater Yellowstone Fire Regimes by Mid-21st Century," *Proceedings of the National Academy of Sciences of the United States of America*, July 25, 2011 (online), www.pnas.org/.

Wikipedia, "Exceptionally Cold Winters," "Grand Canyon of the Yellowstone," and "History of Wolves in Yellowstone," http://en.wikipedia.org/.

Yellowstone National Park, "Aquatic Ecology," "Hydrothermal Features and How They Work," "Weather," "Winter Count Shows Decline in Northern Elk Herd Population," "Yellowstone Bison," and "Yellowstone Cutthroat Trout Preservation," www.nps.gov/.

YellowstoneNationalPark.com, "Geysers—Upper Geyser Basin," www.yellowstone nationalpark.com/.

The author conducted interviews for this chapter with the following:

Linda Miller, spokesperson, Yellowstone National Park.

Tom Olliff, National Park Service landscape coordinator, Great Northern Landscape Conservation Cooperative, Bozeman, MT.

Stephen Saunders, president, Rocky Mountain Climate Organization, Louisville, CO.

CHAPTER 10: GOING UNDER

Marjory Stoneham Douglas, *The Everglades: River of Grass* (New York: Rinehart & Company, 1947).

Everglades National Park, "Birds," "Defender of the Everglades," "Fishes," and "People," www.nps.gov/.

Justin Gillis, "As Glaciers Melt, Science Seeks Data on Rising Seas," *New York Times,* November 13, 2010.

Intergovernmental Panel on Climate Change, "Climate Change 2007: Synthesis Report."

Eli Kintisch, "Caribbean Coral Die-Off Could Be Worst Ever," *ScienceNOW,* October 14, 2010, http://news.sciencemag.org/.

Rachel Loehman and Greer Anderson, "Understanding the Science of Climate Change: Talking Points—Impacts to the Gulf Coast," *Natural Resource Report,* NPS/NRPC/NRR—2010/210, National Park Service, Fort Collins, CO.

Science Daily, "Global Sea-Level Rise at the End of the Last Ice Age Interrupted by Rapid 'Jumps,'" December 4, 2010, www.sciencedaily.com/.

South Florida Natural Resources Center, Everglades National Park, "Climate Change and South Florida's National Parks—Portrait of a Changing Landscape," Fact sheet.

———. "Potential Ecological Consequences of Climate Change in South Florida and the Everglades," 2008 Literature Synthesis, Resource Evaluation Report, SFNRC Technical Series 2009, 1.

U.S. Geological Survey Gulf of Mexico Integrated Science, "Sea-Level Changes," http://gulfsci.usgs.gov/.

U.S. Geological Survey South Florida Information Access, "The South Florida Environment—A Region Under Stress," http://sofia.usgs.gov/.

Wikipedia, "Lake Okeechobee" and "Thermal Expansion," http://en.wikipedia.org/.

The author conducted interviews for this chapter with the following:

Stephen Davis, wetlands ecologist, Everglades Foundation, Palmetto Bay, FL.

Pete Frezza, research manager, Florida Audubon Society Tavernier Science Center, Everglades Region, Tavernier, FL.

Matt Patterson, inventory and monitoring coordinator, South Florida Caribbean Network, National Park Service.

Leonard Pearlstine, landscape ecologist, Everglades National Park.

EPILOGUE

"2010 the Hottest Year on Record," ABC News, January 21, 2011, www.abc.net.au/.

Juliet Eilperin, "2010 Hottest Climate Year on Record, NASA Says," *Washington Post,* December 10, 2010.

Fiona Harvey, "Worst Ever Carbon Emissions Leave Climate on the Brink," *Guardian,* May 29, 2011, www.guardian.co.uk/.

Jack Hedin, "An Almanac of Extreme Weather," *New York Times,* November 27, 2010.

Scott Horsley, "In 2012 GOP Race, Climate Policy Is a Non-Issue," National Public Radio, June 21, 2011, www.npr.org/.

Alok Jha, "Copenhagen Climate Summit: Five Possible Scenarios for our Future Climate," *Guardian,* December 18, 2009, www.guardian.co.uk/.

Clifford Krauss, "In Global Forecast, China Looms Large as Energy User and Maker of Green Power," *New York Times,* November 9, 2010.

Patrick McGeehan, "It Adds Up: This Was New York's Hottest Summer," *New York Times,* August 31, 2010.

National Oceanic and Atmospheric Administration, "NOAA: 2010 Tied For Warmest Year on Record," January 12, 2011, www.noaanews.noaa.gov/.

New York Times, "In Climate Denial, Again," editorial, October 17, 2010.

Solar Feeds, "Climate Change Takes Its Toll on Insurers in 2010," January 4, 2011, www.solarfeeds.com/.

The author conducted interviews for this chapter with the following:

Daniel B. Fagre, biologist and program coordinator, U.S. Geological Survey Northern Rocky Mountain Science Center, Glacier Field Station, West Glacier, MT.

Jon Jarvis, director, National Park Service.

Nathan Stephenson, research ecologist, Sequoia and Kings Canyon Field Station, U.S. Geological Survey Western Ecological Research Center, Three Rivers, CA.